THEY'RE NOT GONE

A collection of true stories from people reunited with their loved ones who've passed away.

Join them in celebrating the moments that Psychic Medium Ricky Wood helped them reconnect and their remarkable stories of realization that their loved ones' spirits are still very much alive

A.P. MORRIS

Outskirts Press, Inc.
Denver, Colorado

THEY'RE
NOT
GONE

To Aunt Miz —
Because you
recieved your own
sign in the pink
ribbon left in
your shoe.
Love, Mathy

Christmas
2009

Maryliz Clark
18 Mindy Dr.
Moorestown, NJ 08057

To my brother, Craig… I love you.

Acknowledgements

Warmest thanks to Janet McGaurn, Darlene Jones, Melissa McConnell, Greta Reimann, Stacey Carlitz, Carla Falcone, Erin Grieco, Shawn Detterline, Deanna Dicampli, Barbara Hawkins, Mathy Downing, Debbie Siple and her siblings. To each of you, thank you for opening your hearts and sharing your memories with me. I am honored that you entrusted me to tell your stories.

A special thanks to my Editor, Jenetha McCutcheon of Quill Editorial Services, for her superb editing skills and belief in this book.

The most important thank you to Ricky Wood, for without you, there would be no stories to tell. You are an angel here on Earth.

To my friends and family who have encouraged and supported me throughout this, thank you. To my Dad, I love you.

Last but never least, to my beautiful daughter Cassandra – you are everything to me and I love you more than I can express in words.

Table of Contents

Introduction

Tragedy is a part of life. Chances are most of us have experienced a loss that has shaken us to our very core. Death is inevitable, yet most of us fear it more than any other event in our lives. This is especially true when it happens unexpectedly or in a way that we find particularly gruesome. These events change our lives and make us question just what happens when we die.

Different religions and upbringings have the most powerful effect on what we believe happens to us after our souls leave our bodies. These beliefs have given some peace and hope. Depending on the circumstances that surround a particular death, we may be exceptionally uneasy and worried about our loved ones' afterlife. Dealing with the aftermath of suicide or similar loss can emotionally paralyze those who are left behind.

I personally have experienced such a loss and after sixteen years have found peace. During a psychic medium connection through Ricky Wood, I found my long lost brother and at last have been able to move on. My story is just one of the many touching and freeing experiences that he has facilitated. After hearing so many of them, I felt it was necessary to share these experiences with others.

These true and moving stories are sure to bring you to tears. They are indisputably authentic connections that prove when our loved ones pass, they are not just gone. They long to reconnect with us as much as we do them so that we are able to move on. Join me in celebrating these miraculous moments. Find the serenity in realizing that we are not without those we miss. They live on, not just in our hearts and memories.

Ricky's intuitive gifts have changed all who have been lucky enough to have an experience with him. He has given us hope, peace, and joy. His talents have allowed us to talk to our deceased loved ones again. We've found comfort in the fact that they are still with us and that we weren't abandoned abruptly.

Ricky, thank you for being such a beautiful human being, your never-ending heart has healed so many. Your humbling gifts have changed our lives and we are forever indebted to you. It is in the rare few like you that love and mercy unequivocally exist.

Join me in celebrating the healing of those whom Ricky has touched. To each and every person who took the time to share his or her story, thank you for opening up your heart to me so I could share your story. Every one is a testament to all that we as a society find difficult to comprehend.

It is my sincere hope that everyone who reads this book will find peace and heal from his or her losses. Most importantly, I want them to realize that they haven't lost because they enjoyed the gift of sharing in their loved ones' lives then and now.

Whether you know it or not, they are still with you today. Our spirits do not vanish with physical death. As Ricky describes it, "They merely exist on a different plane."

They're Not Gone.

1

Meet Ricky Wood

Ricky Wood, the psychic medium who facilitated these reconnections, is just a regular guy. A family man, he enjoys cooking, watching the history channel, and reading comic books. It just so happens that he can "hear" from spirits that are no longer in a physical body. To many it may seem strange, but to Ricky and his family, it is "normal."

In the following interview and after each story, you will get to know how he sees the "big picture," as he answers questions regarding his abilities, spirits, and what he believes happens when we die.

Q & A with Ricky

How did you know you had this ability to hear from spirits that had crossed over?

"Well, sometimes I would see, sometimes I would hear. One time that I recall was when my aunt died when I was in my teen or preteen years. I remember that I was sitting in the kitchen eating something and everyone had either gone to the funeral or something related that I hadn't gone to. Looking out of my left eye, I saw her standing in the living room. But when I turned my head to get a full view, she was gone. So I just kept eating and was just like, whatever."

Was that the first experience you had?

"Well, no. When I was six, I was lying in bed. As a little kid, you know, you're used to seeing stuff all the time, or at least I thought that was normal to see those things. I woke up in the middle of the night, and although there wasn't a lot of light, I saw people. I was scared but not enough to hide my head under the pillow. I remember a man with a fedora walking from my bedroom door to the edge of my bed. Then I saw a revolutionary war soldier walking to the edge of my bed. All of these people just walking to the edge of my bed. And once they got to the edge of my bed they would disappear."

When did you realize that this was not "normal?"

"Well, you have to understand with my mother and aunts and the Hispanic and Catholic upbringing that I had, there was always something goofy. Like my mother would talk about spirits and say things. My aunt too, so I never really thought it was odd when I was younger. I thought *they* were odd but I never thought *it* was odd."

How did you start doing mediumship or allowing spirits to give messages through you?

"After casually doing psychic readings on the side for a while, I did some channeling, which is allowing a spirit to speak through you. Because it was very draining, I pretty much stopped doing it.

Mediumship is picking up on the vibration of what you feel or hear in your head about a spirit and relaying the information. I don't remember exactly when I started doing mediumship, I think it was sometime in the mid-nineties. It started when I began to do more psychic readings and I'd get a feeling about something. For example it may happen like this, I'd be doing a reading and feel like someone was beside me and they would be holding their chest but they would have the most bizarre looking red shoes on. I would relay this and the person in front of me would say, "Oh my God, my father used to wear red clown shoes and he died of a heart attack." That validated what I was feeling, and afterwards I began trusting the information more. Then one day, a friend of an old business partner asked me to 'show her what I did.' So I told her that I felt like her father wanted to talk to her. She clammed up and wouldn't say anything else. Later my old friend and business partner told me that I really needed to watch what I said to people because her father had died the week before. He told me he didn't know what it was that I was doing, but that I better be careful. Since I sometimes took his opinions as fatherly advice, I stopped doing it for a while."

How did you start doing psychic readings & mediumship as your full-time job?

"In the past, I hadn't focused on doing them as a career. I used to work in a vitamin store and business wasn't good. And there were people that knew I did psychic readings as well. Some of them would conveniently show up to 'talk' and they were the only people coming in. It got to the point that the store wasn't bringing in any money. I'd used every penny I had to try and keep it afloat. But the phone would always ring for a reading. Through praying and journaling, I kept asking for help. Finally, I asked God if doing psychic readings and stuff was what I was supposed to do, please help me do it to the best of my ability to help people. Two weeks later, the store closed."

Do you think that you resisted doing psychic readings and mediumship as your career for so long because it was weird and you were afraid of being shunned?

"It is weird. Listen, I've always been a little off center, but I wanted to be as normal as anyone else. I wanted to date girls, go here, go there, sit at a dinner table and get along with everyone and not have to worry about someone asking **"So, you talk to dead people**?" But then I met my other half, Amy. She told me I had to do what I love. And I realized that I loved being a psychic and a medium.

There were some people who shunned me, but I found that anyone who ever really cared about me stuck by me no matter what. Those people are still in my life today."

When you are doing a mediumship session for someone and a spirit comes through, how do you get the information? Do you hear it like you hear me talking to you now?

"It really depends on the session and the spirit who is trying to work with me. There are some spirits that you can just feel. You can feel their personalities, you know what they're like, and they are very, very strong in that respect. There are times when I hear a word clearly. But it doesn't seem auditory like when you are standing five feet away from me and you say "Jonathon" loud and clear. It's more that I feel it on the inside. Like when you're thinking to yourself. You may be thinking about your kid or your dog, but you don't speak your thoughts."

So it's like a knowing versus a hearing or a seeing?

"Yes ma'am, however you would like to translate it."

Do you believe that there is a separate place called "heaven" and "hell" that spirits go to after their physical bodies die?

"This is how I feel. There is a place that is in the light. You can call it heaven, you can call it Cleveland, you can call it whatever you want. There are people there who care about you, who love you, and who know to look for you when you pass, and that transition happens. I get a sense when I'm doing work that those others bring you in. They are the ones that go, 'Hey, Jonathon, over here! Here we are honey, come on by.' So the transition is easier for them, especially people who expect to go there.

Now, the guy who has been murdering people, robbing banks, you name it, this guy is the sludge of the earth. Based upon his religious belief, (and I really believe it is based upon the belief the person has when they die) they will avoid the light; they won't look towards the light."

Because they think that they will get in trouble?

"Sometimes they think they will get in trouble, or they think there is no place like that. So what might happen is, let's say that Bob Smith was a really bad guy. He was horrible, didn't want to deal, he was just mean, mean, mean. So, he dies and he doesn't know what to do, and there is just kind of an empty space for him. Now, if Grandma Martha and some other people are there, they're like, *'Bob Smith get your butt over here now! You are coming to the light and there is a lot that we need to talk about!'* So that's how I feel.

However, if this was a lonely person, someone who didn't have that support, they are kind of not tuned in. So they have a tendency to just walk around and be displaced. If they are a drug addict or alcoholic, they may have a tendency to go towards something that emulates that. I'm still learning all the time. This isn't an exact science. That's the feeling I get."

So are there earthbound spirits because what they believe here on Earth while in a body is what the spirit believes when it first leaves the body?

"Yeah, I mean if you were a devout Muslim and Jesus Christ appeared in front of you in the light, you are going to freak out and you might not go there. So what I believe happens is that the people who are Muslim who are caretakers, would greet you and say, 'This is how the process works. This is how we are going to go about it. This is how you will walk in. And this is how we are going to reunite you.' I mean, I think it is fairly odd that we have such an expansive world with so many religions and dogmas and that *only one* is right."

From your experience, do you feel like when the body dies and a spirit passes, does it gain some type of enlightenment or knowledge? For example, if Jonathon was racist or unkind and he passes and sees how he was, does he change? Do only certain people change? How does that work?

"What happens once they get into the doorway, **I do not know**. However, I do believe that when a spirit tries to communicate with someone else, it will show those aspects of its personality that it had on earth so that the person can cue in. So if Aunt

Mildred was a drunk, racist, racecar driver and she comes through timidly and quietly saying that everything's ok, we are wonderful, we love you, the person getting the reading isn't going to get it or understand because they won't recognize her. So spirits have the tendency to show who they were as the person knows them. I believe that heaven is not just a place of apple pie and ice cream because eventually you'd get pretty bored of apple pie and ice cream throughout eternity."

So you think that we go to a place where you may understand things that you didn't understand while here in a physical body on earth?

"Right. It is a place of learning; it is a place of betterment. It may feel very much like heaven because you don't have that body and the pain and suffering that goes along with having a body. The amount of judgment is reduced to nil. You know, no one gets to judge you. They just don't. What I get is that they may show you. Like alright, the crazy thing is that Hitler, I believe, might get to go to heaven. Now, he might have to stand in line and apologize to six million people one at a time, but he'd get to go. Now this is part of my belief system, so it is not something that was told to me. The feeling I get is that the light is very non-judgmental."

2
Ketchup

"A dog? Everyone has a dog when they're little. Tell me something that only she would know," Ricky said appearing to be talking to himself. He wasn't looking at me. His head was down and his hands remained on the steering wheel in the ten and two position, gripping it as if holding on for dear life.

"What are you talking about?" I asked a little spooked.

"It's your brother Amy. He's showing me a black dog you two had when you were little," he said without looking at me.

I replied, "Well, we had a Doberman when..."

"SSSHHH!" Ricky said as he cocked his head to the side listening as hard as he could. The car grew quiet and my head began to race. Is it really Craig? I wondered.

Parts of me died that day with Craig. He basically raised me until I was five years old because our mother was an alcoholic. After she abandoned us, we moved in with my father. We always relied on each other to not feel so alone. We understood each other. He was more than just a typical brother. I felt safe with him; I thought that he'd always protect me. Since the day he died, I've felt very alone.

I'd found out Ricky was psychic one day after casually knowing him for almost a year. He had given me a reading and mentioned things he couldn't have known about me. I was impressed, but I didn't think he was a medium like John Edwards. I had read books by John Edwards and wished that I could afford a session with him.

Ricky and I were dating now, and had just come from visiting my brother's grave. It was the first time I'd taken him there. We were parked outside of a bookstore. My head was racing and I was scared, yet excited. I never imagined that I would hear from my brother again especially through Ricky.

After another half a minute or so, Ricky turned and looked at me questioningly. "**Ketchup**?" he asked appearing confused. I repeated "ketchup" to myself as my brain began a number of memory searches. I was transformed back to my childhood. I quickly made the connection and was overcome with emotion. My chest heaved, the damn broke and the flood of tears began.

"Are you OK honey?" Ricky asked panicked.

"Is he alright, is he in pain?" I asked frantically. I felt sixteen again. The day I heard, "Craig shot himself – he's dead." I was hungry for answers and I wanted to know if he was ok. Was the religious doctrine I'd been taught incorrect? Was he in hell for committing suicide?

"Is he happy?" I shouted needing to know.

"He's very happy Amy," Ricky stated soothingly. "He's more than ok, I feel like he's all wrapped in a cocoon of love and peace." Ricky said as his eyes shined brightly.

"Oh, thank you," I said through a flood of fresh tears. My fears for the last sixteen years were fading. He wasn't damned for all of eternity and laboring in the trenches of hell for what he did.

"What does "ketchup" mean Amy?" Ricky asked uncertain of his message.

"My Dad used to call him names when he got mad at him," I said. A picture came into my head of one of the scenarios. My dad would tell my brother to go get him a screwdriver or whatever. Craig wouldn't be able to find it. My dad would yell, "Come on Craig, you're so damn slow you're just like ketchup!" The name eventually became just Ketchup whenever he took too long and he tested dad's patience.

Ricky didn't respond to my explanation. After another minute he said, "I'm sorry Amy, I didn't mean to upset you."

"Well, if he's not in pain or sad then why did he tell me something so negative?" I inquired skeptically.

"He knows that you equate his death with sadness and your father," he said without hesitation. "He knew the only way you would believe it was him was to bring up something only the two of you knew about your father, something you'd never told anyone."

"That makes sense," I thought, Craig had killed himself on Father's Day.

"He's sorry," Ricky continued, "That he hurt you and especially your dad. He was in so much pain here and it was time for him to go, he's very happy now. He's seen you and Cassandra. He says your daughter is as beautiful as you. He's in another life now, his energy is around children with Autism." Ricky smiled, "No Amy he's not in pain – he loves it, he's loved and happy."

My brain was on fire! It felt like circuits were connecting at lighting speed. I'd felt his presence while working. I worked with children diagnosed with autism. I wasn't sure how that had happened because it was not what I'd gone to school for or the career path I'd thought I would follow. Yet, I felt so comfortable being with these children. It was as if I had an unspoken bond with them. I seemed some-how feel as if I knew them or innately understood them even if they couldn't speak. It all seemed to be making sense.

"Go on," I said feeling exhilarated.

"He's proud of the wonderful mother you are," Ricky said softly. "He also wants you to stop being sad and angry, at yourself, your dad and the whole world. Let the past go and enjoy your future, ev-erything will be ok. He loves you Amy," Ricky said teary-eyed.

Ricky's hands slowly let go of the steering wheel. "Wow," he said, "that was intense." I came back to reality. I wasn't sure how long we had been sitting in the parking lot of the bookstore. I felt like I could run a marathon. I was so elated. Craig was ok and sixteen years of worry seem to evaporate like rain on hot black top on a steamy summer day. It felt surreal.

I didn't want it to be over, but I could see how much it had drained Ricky. He looked exhausted. "Are you ok?" I asked concerned.

"Yeah, it was just draining and it took a lot of energy," he said.

As he rested for a few moments, I marveled at the love and peacefulness I felt surrounding me as my entire soul seemed to be smiling. Everything was ok. I had always felt that it was impossible that someone as good and kindhearted as Craig deserved to go to hell. He was the kindest person I'd ever met. The one and only cruel thing he'd ever done was his last act.

I seemed to be seeing a bigger picture than I thought was possible. Almost as if we as humans are unable to grasp the grandness of what exists beyond our life now.

As Ricky seemed to be regaining his strength, we got out of the car and slowly made our way to the entrance of the bookstore. "Thank you Ricky, that was the greatest gift I've ever received," I said as I put my hand in his. "You've just healed sixteen years of pain. I will always be grateful."

I'd never told a soul about Ketchup. Even my best and oldest friends were amazed by my story. To prove the authenticity of his presence to me, Craig definitely picked something that could not be disputed. It's not something that you tell people. Although it has a negative connotation, I was happy that he chose something so obscure. I've always been a natural skeptic, so if I was told something that I'd ever repeated, I would have probably second-guessed or doubted the authenticity of the reading. I wouldn't have accepted something that is common in children's lives. Knowing me so well, Craig and Ricky made sure that I didn't doubt the connection or discount my message.

At that moment I didn't realize the impact it would have on my life -- the weights that had been lifted and how in the coming years, I would let go of the pain and embrace life. I'm not angry anymore. I don't feel like life has been unfair to me and I've let go of the pain that encompassed me. I've built a friendship with my dad knowing that his pain has followed him everyday since that Father's Day sixteen years ago. I love and appreciate him for the great man that he is today. All of which would not be possible without this experience with Ricky.

I had real trust issues and that's why I believe Ricky was the one to deliver this information to me. I was so full of distrust and sadness that I don't think I would have allowed just anyone to come near those still raw scars.

I had no idea how much hearing from my

brother would leave me open to receiving messages on my own. About a year after the reconnection, I unexpectedly received a message through a writing experience. I've always loved to write, especially when I wanted to rid myself of sad and anxious feelings.

After watching a music video on TV that told a story of suicide, I was moved to pick up a pen and paper. It felt almost as if a force took over. My hand moved fervently down the page, scrawling almost illegible words. I wasn't thinking of them, they just came quickly and unexpectedly. Once I finished, I went back and read it as if reading it for the first time. I had no idea what it said.

Feeling as if I was buzzing with a thousand volts of electricity, I read what appeared to be song lyrics.

FORGIVE ME

CHORUS

Forgive me Forgive me for taking my life on your day
Forgive me Forgive me for taking my life in your name
Please, forgive me for leaving a cloud on your day

I hated you; you broke me I thought that's what you deserved

You gave me my freedom to go on to the next
world
I realize you were just a little frightened boy
You didn't mean to break my spirit down
You didn't know what to do with my sister or I

Don't cry no more my tears are part of the rain
I'm helping the others learn to get with the game
You are the one I need to thank the most
Without you without you I would've never known
this part
You have become the most giving and loving
friend
Don't forget I love you for being a stronger man
My life helped you see what others can't
Don't stop giving you're my hero now
You gave me life and we showed each other how
We were suppose to do for the greater good

I miss you I can't wait to see you one of these days
I can say my father is a changed man
I can't take back what that day in June did
Just know you are the man I strive to be...for
You love so deeply and now I hope you can see...
so Please...

I eventually presented them to my father as a
gift for Christmas from Craig. I'd never written lyrics prior to this incident. As beautiful as they are,
I cannot take credit for they are a direct message
from son to father.

Here is what I have to say about my experiences with Ricky:

"In that short twenty minutes in my car that evening, my life was completely transformed. Knowing that my brother and mother are still very much alive, I've finally begun to live *my* life. Now I can feel the love they have for me that never died, that can't die. I feel less alone, I no longer fear "death," and I am forever changed.

I am thankful everyday for Ricky, not only because he gave me a priceless gift that completely changed my life, but for the true compassion and love he feels for everyone. He has the biggest heart of anyone I've ever met. Treating his abilities with true humbleness, Ricky is aware that he has been given this gift and he honors it by giving to each and every person he meets. His pure selflessness is beautiful and inspiring. Ricky, thank you for being you."

A.P. Morris

Craig on Dad's motorcycle

Craig with little sister Amy.

Craig Patrick Morris

Q & A with Ricky:

In some religions, it is taught that those who commit suicide go to hell. Based on your experiences as a medium, what do you think?

"I think that 'hell' is of one's own making so it really depends on their belief system before they die."

So you don't think they actually go to a place with fire and brimstone?

"No, I don't get that at all. But some people, because of their guilt or shame or whatever they have going on, seem to have the tendency to separate themselves from the source -- the light. Not all of them do it. There are kids that have committed suicide and their grandparents beckon them into the light, and then they are all in the light and everyone seems ok there."

Then do you see any difference in what happens to a person after they die regardless of their death being from suicide versus death from a heart attack or car accident?

"I don't see much difference in it other than the amount of guilt that someone would have when they kill themselves. For a person who dies in a car accident who may have a loving wife waiting on the other side, it may be quite simple. But someone who has committed suicide, who doesn't feel connected to friends, family, or loved ones, can still have that feeling when they die. So they may avoid the light or going towards it. Kind of like keeping your back turned and your head down."

Do you personally think that suicide is part of a pre-drawn plan for a spirit, or do you think that it is a mental illness that develops from the mind or external factors on Earth?

"Well first, I'm not a doctor, so I don't really know that. Based upon my limited knowledge, because it is limited, I think it is rare to have a pre-ordained plan to kill oneself."

Do you think that certain people are sent here to kill themselves for a reason, such as bringing about change, or do you think that suicide is a cop out?

"I think they are here to bring about change in some ways; however, in many cases there are better ways to do it other than committing suicide. Suicide rarely comes from a place of love or self-love. It rarely comes from a place to help mankind. It is self-inflicted; it is about the self. It does not mean that those people are bad people *at all*; it just means that they are hurting in such a way that they can't reach past that point to do something different. Now, suicide has an impact on family and others all over the place, but I think (and remember this is just what I think and feel) people who commit suicide, depending on who their guides are, who is waiting for them in the light, and how willing they are to see it will mean their connection to it. There are young people who have committed suicide and they are fine. There are other people who have committed suicide and you can tell they are in the light. You get a good happy feeling. Once again, it depends on your belief system, if you believe in God of some kind, or the light of some kind, or the love of relatives, then there's a good chance you'll be ok."

Do you think that people who commit suicide are looked upon at physical death as being wrong?

"From what I understand, there is no major counsel that sits and judges these people. There are guides, helpers, teachers, instructors, loved ones who may say, 'Killing yourself didn't help you achieve anything.' There are different circumstances. If someone is dying from cancer or something like that, it may be different. They are in the anticipation of dying and they are thinking about the light or heaven or loved ones. It always depends on the person, and most importantly, their beliefs. Many people who kill themselves are in such a state of sadness, or if they are on drugs or something, they are in such a state that they are not thinking about the light, they are just trying to end the pain."

In this "Ketchup" story, Craig told me that he was sorry for what he did. Does that mean it was a mistake, he should not have done it, or he was wrong?

"I was getting that; first of all, they would be

sorry like anyone else. If they cared about you and loved you and knew you were in pain because of it, they would be sorry. They would definitely be sorry. It's what they chose at that time. Usually, it is a state of regret when they're done. I think he wishes that he thought there was another way but at that point, he didn't know of another way to end his pain."

Do you see any connection at all of his death being a necessity for all involved to grow, or do you think it was all about him?

"It affected all involved, but I don't think he realized what that effect would be. Or maybe his soul knew it would create an effect. But I still believe he always had other choices. It doesn't mean that he was bad, at all, it just means that maybe on the other side with help he would say, "Wow, maybe if I stuck around more I would have created something different. I could have made it better for myself or for my sister." Or he felt so stuck, he had no choice. There is mental illness. Depression is depression."

So you don't think that it is really looked upon as bad and shouldn't have happened or it was right and should of happened, but more like it is what happened, it is what it is, and it's all about how you deal with it?

"Right. What do you want to learn from this? You know, it is all different. I mean if someone is in a war and there are eighteen combatants coming up ready to torture you, you may kill yourself.

That's considered suicide but that's a little different. You hadn't been planning it and planning it. I think a lot of people who have thoughts of suicide have thoughts of depression. When they are feeling down, they feel like there is no way out. I think we have all felt that to some degree."

I described a time when I thought Craig gave a message to our dad through me with the song lyrics "Forgive Me." Does everyone have the ability to hear from spirits and see, hear, or write messages from them?

"I do think sometimes you definitely get a message and sometimes your love and their love for you creates a feeling. It creates an energy. Everything is about energy. So love doesn't die, it just can't. They care about you. I don't always know that someone would always say 'here are the lyrics for your song,' however, they may be sending the message; *'you inspire so many people through writing, so why aren't you writing.'* They're not muses all the time. If you feel better about yourself and you feel uplifted, then yes, their energy would be *'hey, why don't you write.'*"

Do you doubt that it was a message he wanted to get to his father?

"I don't know because it didn't happen through me, but the feeling I get is that he does not want his father to suffer, so however that came to be. I think it is a beautiful thing because once someone gets clear, they can help someone else feel clear if they can. And you have to remember too that the person has to be in the space of being willing and wanting to hear it."

Do you think everyone has the ability? They just need to be clear, open, and wanting?

"Right, all of it. I think that if people sat still long enough, they would feel the love of someone. I think people just want to know that the essence of their loved one is still around."

And the essence is still around?

"Right."

3
Old Friends

Some of us have had our own personal experiences with seeing, speaking, or hearing from those who have passed. Many times we do not need a psychic medium to facilitate these reunions if we are open to them. However, when we are very close to a person or situation, we don't always have the clarity we need to really listen. Fear can be paralyzing and it inevitably blocks our own abilities to receive messages.

Dr. Janet McGaurn grew up in a family that embraced spirituality. She came from a family of chiropractors that innately knew that health encompassed more than the physical body. She learned that the mind, body, and spirit were all intertwined. Janet followed in her father's footsteps as a chiropractor to help others heal. Her mother taught her that spirituality is who we are and that religion was merely a man-made attempt at explaining it. Throughout her life, Janet has continued to study spirituality, religion, and the unknown in hopes of validating what she knew deep down to be true. She has struggled with trusting her own instincts and medical intuition in her work and personal life.

About four years prior to meeting Ricky, Janet had her own personal experience with a visit from her deceased Uncle Eddie. They had a very close relationship in which he looked after her much like an older brother. She was staying at her parent's home in the bedroom he died in when he spoke with her. Awakened from her sleep, Janet saw a red and white flashing light radiating from the corner of the room. It was coming from her cell phone. Janet couldn't understand how this was happening because it didn't have the capability to flash red and white. An overwhelming feeling of her uncle's presence enveloped her as she saw a picture in her mind of the red and white afghan she had made him years earlier.

On another visit, she actually saw him as if he was a white swirling gaseous like form. He had spoken to and comforted her with the message that everything would be ok with what was going on in her life at the time.

After these reunions, she was certain of the fact that everyone lives on even after death and that they have the ability to communicate with you. Although Janet was sure of this, she wasn't as accepting of it when she was given the news that her mother could have cancer. Shortly after learning about the possible diagnosis, she was wracked with fear and uncertainty. Janet found herself unable to be comforted by her knowledge of the continued existence of our spirits after death. Her mother was staying with her while she was going through numerous tests and doctors appointments. Janet was worried sick and unable to find any peace of mind.

Ricky greatly helped her by giving her an unexpected message as she adjusted his spine. He lay down on the table and she began working on his back. "Who is the lady... who's your mother's sister?" Ricky suddenly asked her.

Janet replied, "My mother doesn't have a sister."

He continued, "No, no, this woman looks exactly like your mother. Everyone thought they were sisters... they dressed the same way and everything." Janet had stopped adjusting him and stood back as he continued adamantly.

Ricky quickly took his hands up to the sides of his head and began motioning. Janet watched unable to move. She was enthralled with his drive to have her recognize the visitor trying to communicate through him. He swept his hands back from his face and finished with an upward motion in the back of his head.

"She wore her hair like this," he said as he continuously swept his hands back and up as if trying to create a picture for her to see. "I also see a white... a white ribbon, white feather, or something white in her hair!"

Janet froze. She felt chills cover her entire body.

"Oh my God, that is my mom's friend Tony!" she said. "She died of cancer, a brain tumor, oh about twenty years ago," she continued as the pieces fell into place. "I remember my parents wedding picture. Tony was her maid of honor and they both wore white. My mom was wearing a white feather hat!" Janet clearly saw the picture of the two of them from that day so many years ago.

"Yes, that's her," Ricky said. "She's smiling and nodding…she's acknowledging that it is her."

Janet's eyes began tearing. A flood of relief enveloped her body. She was surprised because she hadn't known Tony that well, only having visited with her a couple of times during her childhood. Tony and her husband had moved to Arizona when Janet was very young. Yet, somehow she knew unequivocally that it was Tony. It was as if the three of them were sitting in the room and Ricky was merely interpreting for her. Janet was tingling all over and wishing her mother were there.

Ricky continued, "She wants you to tell your mom not to worry, she has nothing to worry about, everything will be fine. She also wants you to know when it's your mother's time that she will greet her, she will be waiting for her and she will greet her," he continued in a soothing voice.

Janet felt the weight of fear being lifted from her shoulders. No matter what the tests showed, her mother would be ok. The heart-wrenching thoughts of watching her mother suffer in pain through a long bout of cancer dissipated instantaneously as if

Tony had taken them with her.

Janet drove home after work with an entirely different outlook than when she'd left that morning. Her mother didn't have cancer and she would be fine! She felt light as she strode into her house to talk to her mom. Janet was eager to put her mother's fears to rest as hers had been earlier that day. Her mother knew about Ricky and his abilities. She knew that her mom would be open to Ricky's message, but she wanted to retell the events as they unfolded so she could experience it as she had.

"Mom, I had the coolest thing happen today," Janet began. "Ricky came in for an adjustment. When I began working on him he suddenly started asking me who my mother's sister was. I told him you didn't have a sister." Janet continued excitedly as her mother's face lit up and she listened intently. "Then he said that everyone thought you were sisters and that you both looked alike and dressed the same way! He started pulling his hands back and up and saying that she wore her hair like this. He said something about a white ribbon or something white in the hair. It was…"

"Tony," her mother said before she could finish.

"Yes!" Janet squealed. "It was her mom! When he was talking I remembered your wedding picture, and you had a white feather hat on, and the sides of her hair were pulled up and back! She said everything was going to be ok, and to tell you not to worry!"

"Oh, Janet I have chills everywhere," her mother said breathlessly. Janet watched as her mother began wrapping her arms around herself. Suddenly, she cried out, "HHUUHH! I feel her, Tony's here, oh my god – it almost feels like she's hugging me!" her mother said as tears began streaming down her cheeks. She didn't fight them or try to wipe them away. As Janet watched her hugging herself she realized that Tony was indeed hugging her mom trying to comfort her.

"She's giving you a hug mom," Janet said confidently. As they stood in the kitchen of Janet's house, they both felt the love and comfort of Tony. Janet and her mother embraced and their fears and unrest rolled away along with their tears. Peace filled the entire room.

Janet believes that the message was given and interpreted exactly the way it was supposed to be at that time. Her mother really lived. She didn't wait to die. She embraced life to a great extent because, through Ricky, Tony had given her peace of mind. It was not a time without pain and discomfort; however, she didn't spend it living in fear of cancer or death.

A year and three months later, Janet said goodbye to her mother. Although grief-stricken and mourning her loss, Janet smiled to herself as she pictured Tony welcoming her mom to the other side. After twenty-five years the childhood friends were together again.

Initially, Janet was confused. All of the biopsies

had come back negative. Her mom had *not* been diagnosed or treated for cancer. She had thought that the message she'd received from Ricky had told her that her mom did **not** have cancer and that she would live forever.

As Janet recalled the day Tony came through, she realized that messages could be interpreted so differently. Tony had said that she would be there to greet her when it was her mother's time. Now that gave her great comfort; however, she had discounted that at the time. She thought if her mom did not have cancer, she wouldn't die, and Tony would be greeting her many years from now. Her initial interpretation was that everything would be ok, her ok, which meant no cancer, no pain, and no death.

Although the loss of her mother continues to be difficult for her, as it is for most people, Janet finds joy in knowing that her mother is with her friend and that she is happy. She laughs talking about the recent session in which her mother and Tony came through together, happily drinking coffee and playing cards. These instances coupled with beautiful memories help her move on. Although her mom is not physically here any longer, Janet knows that she isn't gone.

Here is what Janet has to say about her experiences with Ricky:

"My experiences with Ricky have validated my own intuitive feelings. I have more confidence in what I sense and how I believe I'm being guided. I have more trust in universal intelligence -- God, and I feel more cared for and watched over. I know now that death is truly just a transition that our souls must go through and that we never really die...we just change form."

Dr. Janet McGaurn

Janet's mother Grace on her wedding day with Tony to her left.

Grace Mary McGaurn

Q & A with Ricky

In this story with Dr. Janet McGaurn, you gave her a message while being adjusted. Do you typically find messages coming out when you are not "in session" while going about your everyday life?

"I knew Janet fairly well and we had a close relationship, so there was an understanding that if I needed to say something, I could, but that was with Janet. I've had many experiences on her chiropractic table when she was working on a certain spot on my spine and it releases and sometimes I get information that way. Why? I don't know. But I did trust her a great deal and it was known that I was free to speak. But no, I wouldn't do it with my dentist, or my insurance salesman."

When Tony was telling Janet that her mom would be "OK" do you see or "know" what that means? For example, when she was being told that everything was going to be ok, Janet initially heard ok to mean no cancer, no death. But just over a year later, her mom passed anyway. How do you interpret Ok?

"The message that I got was that she was fine right now -- she's OK. What I felt was that the message was for Janet and her mother not to worry and that needed to be a sense of calm for her. That was what needed to happen for her at that particular moment."

When you are giving information, is it almost like you are just a portal or interpreter, not that you "know" everything that is going to happen?

"Yes. I don't get everything. It's kind of like picking out different smells from a kitchen when someone is cooking. You may smell more rosemary. Then if you concentrate you can smell the lemon, or the chicken. You start to separate all the different smells, like I do with information. And I'm interpreting, so I'm giving them the closest meaning of what I get."

How important do you think "believing" you are ok, whether your current physical existence ends or not, is to enjoying your life here and now on Earth?

"I think if everyone knew that they'd be ok, that everything is going to be alright, they could live their life more fully. Half the problem is that most of us hold on to our own guilt, shame, control issues, and all kinds of stuff. Most people come from a place of fear constantly. They have a fear of losing something, or a fear of not being able to control something, so that usually creates all of their worry. Most people don't like to go with the flow, they can't stand it. I think that is part of the 'hell on Earth' that people deal with. It is kind of funny, but if more people where a little more like Forest Gump, I think it would be a lot better. We all have our own fear base. I think the less fear someone has, the better off they are. We spend most time trying to influence or change an individual, but contentment comes from self-achieved happiness. Your inner core is happy. If someone has a child that is acting up or a spouse or pet that is not doing what they would like them to do, they are unhappy. We all want them do what we want them to do, then we think we'll be happy. It isn't always true."

It seems to be painful for most of us to lose a loved one regardless of how old they are or what they died from. What advice would you give to people when they lose someone who is very important to them on how to live happily without that person's physical presence?

"Just send them love, believe it or not. Not the other way around."

To send the person that died love?

"Yes, to send them love and feelings of your gratitude for your relationship with them. You know I think it is a really good thing to share from your heart how well you are doing. In other words, that you are starting to feel a little better or thanking them for what they taught you."

So look at it in a positive light instead of a negative light?

"Yes, that's the best thing you can do. I think that gives a lot more resolution a lot faster. Speak to them in a way that you love and appreciate them and that they were an important part of your life and that you'll see them soon. But acting as though you don't want them to go and they can't go away and they have to be there by you, that isn't a helping-you-grow scenario. If you're sending worry and you're sending thoughts that you can't make it, you can't get that love back from them because you have a negative barrier up. I mean, everyone has their mourning and grieving process, but sending as much love as you can send is the best thing. Love doesn't die. The aspect of them caring about you can't die, so you know that you are always connected to that. And a way for people to feel that is to send them love. Just send them love, you will get it back."

4

Decisions

Choices that have to be made at the end of one's life can be traumatic —especially when those decisions are left up to the loved one taking care of the dying. This can leave them questioning whether they made the right choice. Wondering whether a different decision may have resulted in the preferred outcome—that their loved one would have lived and still be with them today. Unfortunately, many times this can be emotionally paralyzing and impede any future happiness for the person who had to make the decision.

Darlene Jones, one of the kindest and most nonpretentious people I've ever met, graciously shared her experiences with me. She was left with making a decision about her husband, Dennis, at the end of his life. Although she believed at the time that she was making the right choice, she desperately needed to hear from him that she had done so. Until then, she was unable to find peace.

Darlene and Dennis shared a happy life during their twenty-eight year marriage. Along with two sons, they embraced the joy of living every day to the fullest. They worked hard and played hard, eventually acquiring their dream—a vacation home at a beach in a nearby state. Dennis, a juvenile diabetic, was an outgoing, strong-willed, tell-it-like-it-is kind of man. He was the life of the party and the inspiration and motivation for his family and friends. He didn't allow his disease to hold him back, instead he used it as the reason for finding pleasure in everything he did. Left with low self-esteem and the glass-is-half empty outlook from an extremely difficult and wounding childhood, Darlene saw life differently because of Dennis' perspective. He was always the positive force in her life. He would tell her, "You can do whatever you set your mind to, go get 'em girl!" Dennis gave her what she failed to receive in the early years of life —unconditional love, support, and the tools to believe in herself.

The last few years of Dennis' life were trying. Complications of the diabetes were catching up with him. However, he met all of his tribulations with a positive outlook and the will to go on. Eye implants, kidney failure, losing both legs and part of his hands still weren't enough to defeat his strong spirit. Along with the love and support of Darlene, family and friends, he faced every incident with a tenacity that is rarely seen in most human beings. Darlene took care of him with patience and a meticulousness that reflected her remarkable unconditional love for him.

Raised as a devout Catholic, Darlene believed that one's spirit didn't die along with the body. She also knew that spirits existed because of her own personal experiences with hearing and seeing examples of this in her early childhood. It wasn't until she saw the TV show "Crossing Over," starring John Edwards that she learned that you could communicate with them. Dennis, however, didn't believe in that sort of stuff.

One afternoon he asked her if you went right to heaven when you die. She told him she wasn't sure, but that she was taught that you went to heaven. She wasn't positive about the heaven or hell part, but she believed that you go to a place that is better than this, where you're at peace. She laughed and said, "But I don't know because no one has ever come back and told me."

"If I can, I'll come back and tell you," Dennis said to her surprise.

Peritonitis, a life threatening infection that is common among people with kidney damage, was the final assault on Dennis' body. Darlene didn't believe that it was the end for him. He'd made it through so much and she didn't want this time to be any different. The doctors discussed having him prepare a living will. He told them he trusted Darlene with his life and he didn't need one. She tried to explain the importance of it to Dennis; however, he would not go there. She needed to believe that it was unnecessary; therefore, she didn't push.

When the doctors left the room, Dennis turned to Darlene and said, "You took very good care of me."

She smiled and responded, "Good, then just get better."

"OK, I'll do that," he told her.

Soon afterwards, he had to be transported to a different hospital. During this move, he was accidentally dropped to the floor and began having breathing problems.

The following day, while in the middle of talking to the doctor, he fell back and subsequently was placed on a respirator to keep him alive. They found that he had internal bleeding. The doctors told Darlene they could operate but the chances weren't great. Darlene asked if he would have any happy days left if he had the surgery. The doctor told her no. He informed her that the blood pressure medication was the only thing keeping him alive. If they cut the medicine back slowly, he would just go. She agreed to do it slowly so that he would make it through to the next day. She didn't want him to leave on their son's birthday. She stepped out of the room to say goodbye to the kids at ten of eight. When she returned, the nurse told her that Dennis had passed away.

Darlene was grief-stricken. She immediately began questioning her decision to slowly cut back his medications. A statement that Dennis had jokingly made a while back rang in her ears -- "I never want you to pull the plug on me." Darlene, numb with disbelief, went through the motions after his death. She honored his wishes and had him cremated. She kept his ashes in a box in their home.

Months later, Darlene turned on the television and watched as John Edwards told a woman that she had to let her husband go. That her unwillingness to let him go was keeping him here and that she had to give him permission to move on. Darlene felt as if he was speaking to her. It was a beautiful sunny day. She packed a bag and placed Dennis' box of ashes next to her in the car. Without telling a soul, she drove straight to their beach house. In the last few years of Dennis' life he was unable to go there because there wasn't a hospital close by. She felt that he would want her to let him go there.

It was the perfect evening to say goodbye. There was a light breeze. The moon illuminated the towering lighthouse. The water was calm and inviting. Darlene slowly opened the box trying to steady her shaking hands. She knew it was time as she summoned all of her love for him. As the breeze carried his ashes away, tears cascaded down her cheeks. She felt as if her entire body was encased in concrete. Her soul screamed a sorrowful, "NO – I WANT HIM BACK!" She shuttered with the realization that she couldn't bring him back and she immediately regretted having opened the box.

A few weeks later, Darlene sat in the TV room as she and her husband used to do most evenings. She sat on the couch where she always sat and she stared at the chair where Dennis used to sit. It was empty and so was her heart. She cried and spoke out loud to Dennis. She let out the heartache she felt from her loss. Her chest heaved as she said, "I know that you didn't love me or you wouldn't have left me. I was just your caregiver, that's why you stayed with me. I am so lonely." She wished she were at the beach house so she could feel closer to him.

The phone rang and she pulled herself together to answer it. It was Debbie, her oldest friend. She and her husband, Kevin, were very close to Dennis and Darlene. Debbie hesitantly told her that she had been to a psychic medium that day. She proceeded by telling her she didn't want to freak her out, but she had something she had to tell her. Darlene told her to go on. Debbie told her that Dennis had come through so strong in her reading that a lot of it was about him. He wanted you to get the message so you would go see Ricky yourself. Darlene was ecstatic! She wanted to hear from Dennis that she had made the right decision at the end. That he wasn't mad at her and that he was ok. Her son paid for her to go as a birthday gift.

Two days later, her friend Debbie drove her to her appointment with Ricky. She was so nervous, but she felt like she was being pushed to go. She was scared, yet she needed to know. "Is he mad at me because I told them not to operate and to cut back his medication at the end?" Darlene questioned herself throughout the entire ride.

Ricky began, "Your husband wants you to know

that you don't have to go to your special place to see or visit with him. Does that make sense?" he asked her.

"Yeah, I thought I had to go to our beach house where I put his ashes to be close to him," she responded.

"He wants you to know that he's with you all the time," Ricky said adamantly. "He also wants you to know that he still sits in his recliner when you are on the couch where you two sat in the evenings. He heard you the other night when you were upset and saying he didn't love you or he wouldn't have left and something about him just staying because you took care of him?" Ricky said in a questioning tone as he tilted his head to the side. Darlene felt like she was floating and peacefulness enveloped her body.

"Oh my God! He heard me?" Darlene gasped.

"Yes," Ricky continued, "He heard everything. He wants you to know that he really loves you Darlene, and he didn't stay with you because you took care of him." Tears began welling up in her eyes.

Ricky felt Dennis' urgency to get his message to his wife clearly and concisely "He's sorry that he had to go, but it was his time. He also wants you to know that he won't leave you until you really want him to go, until you're ready," Ricky said as Darlene began to weep again. She felt as if weights were being lifted from her shoulders as she recalled the evening she let his ashes go. The realization that he wasn't gone filled her heart.

"Good, because I'm not ready for him to go."

"He knows that Darlene," Ricky said soothingly. "But he can't stay forever," he added softly.

"I know," she answered, knowing that he was right.

"He also wants you to know that the friends you both had when he was here, are your friends too. They love you for you, not just because you were with him," Ricky said matter-of-factly. Darlene's head was spinning. She was in awe that Ricky was telling her these things that she hadn't told anyone. She had no doubt that she was talking to Dennis and she didn't want it to end.

As Darlene left Ricky's office, she told Debbie that her body felt so light it almost seemed weightless. For the first time since his death, she realized he wasn't just gone. A smiled covered her face, as she felt happy for the first time since she could remember.

Darlene went to bed that evening filled with peace. She didn't ask herself if she'd made the right decision. The day seemed surreal. She could have sworn that she felt as if he was lying in bed next to her.

Darlene has received mixed reviews from some of her family and friends about her experiences with reconnecting with Dennis through Ricky. Some felt that it wasn't a positive in her life because she was not moving on. She wishes that they could understood that this has helped her immensely because without it she feels that she would still be tortured with questioning her decisions. Others see that it has given her peace and is allowing her to move on because she is getting rid of any uncertainty that she had.

During a call to Ricky to schedule another reading, he told her Dennis was saying, "If you'd open yourself up, you wouldn't have to spend your money to talk to him!" Darlene still struggles with letting Dennis go; however, it has gotten easier because she knows that he's not gone.

Here is what Darlene has to say about her experiences with Ricky:

"Meeting Ricky Wood has changed my life in many ways. I have a peace in my life that was never there, not even in my childhood. He has given me faith that my sons' lives will come together in a good and productive way, and that there are many happy times ahead for me."

Darlene Jones

Darlene Jones

Dennis fishing at the beach.

Dennis David Jones

Q & A with Ricky

In this story, Dennis tells his wife that he would come back if he could after passing. Darlene's friend Debbie heard about you and came to you for a session in which Dennis came through to give a message to Darlene. This led to Darlene coming and hearing from Dennis. Do you think this is a coincidence?

"I don't think there are any coincidences. In other words, as long as I've been doing this work, that's what I get. I think coincidences are rare, although every once in a while a cheeseburger is just a cheeseburger; it's just what it is. But usually it is not. It is interesting like I may move my office, or be flying to Arizona, or I'll be in New Jersey and someone will bump into someone else, who bumps into someone else, and I'll be at the right place at the right time."

So do you think that spirits can manifest things or is it because they wanted something so bad? How does that happen?

"I'm sure they nudge people a lot. That's what it feels like."

I know you've said how tiring it can be to change your vibration to be able to communicate with spirits. How hard do you think is it for a spirit to come through and communicate?

"I think they have to learn to match the vibration,

but to tell you the truth, I've never been dead that I remember, so I don't know. But I believe they have to match the vibration of the live human they are communicating with. I sense that it is a bit difficult. Otherwise, it would be crystal clear interpretation all the time."

Dennis said to Darlene in the session that he wouldn't leave until she was ready. Do you think a lot of spirits might hold back and hang around longer because their loved one they left behind is extremely upset and sad?

"Sometimes I think that's it. I don't always think it is the healthiest thing, but yes they do. I felt that Dennis had a very strong attachment to Darlene and the house. You also have to remember that this woman was so full of grief, and she was so close to him that it feels like he would stick around."

What does "stick around" mean? Does it mean that they have crossed over, yet their spirit hasn't moved on and they are still hanging around here?

"Yes. If the energy is very gentle and loving, it feels like they are projecting love from the other side. Then there are other times when it feels like they are right there, in the home. They really haven't moved because they feel so attached to the living that they won't move. Imagine if you were a mother and you had lost your child. The child might be so attached to the mother that the child doesn't move."

I read somewhere that there is a window of opportunity to move on that opens up when you die. (I'm not referring to Dennis. I don't know if he crossed over or not at the time of the reading. You just opened that door for me.) So do you think that people who haven't crossed have the opportunity at a later time?

"I think that the light is not like a door that opens and closes. I think that it is always there. Spirits choose to either go towards it, or they choose not to. Let's say, if you were a kid and your mother was telling you to come into the house. She'd say, *'You need to come in now, Joey; it's time to have dinner.'* You can ignore that for a little while until Mom comes out. Then Dad comes out and tells you, *'Come in the house NOW, dinner is ready.'* You know, I think it's the same way. If there are a lot of people who know you and are a part of your life, they will try and use their energy to draw you in. But there are a lot of lonely people who don't have a lot of family and stuff, and for them, it might be there pet drawing them in."

At the end of their story, Dennis told Darlene that she could hear from him herself and that she didn't need to spend money to come see you to do that. Do you think that it is possible that anyone can receive communication from their loved one?

"Yes, absolutely. Now, you have to remember that most of us are so used to communicating like you and I are communicating right now. So that 'feeling' or 'nudge' might not be enough for them. A lot of people want to hear, you know, 'I AM HERE RIGHT NOW, and so on.' They want a "normal" conversation."

And it's not like that?

"It isn't always like that."

Is it that you have to be more aware?

"I have to tell you this, I think that it is a big mistake for people to think that there is only one way to do it. And I think that confuses people, it bothers them because they want it to be a certain way. Some may come through electronics that start to get affected. Some people get a very direct message. You know God communicates through other people, books, movies, music, all kinds of ways, if you are just willing to listen. I'll tell you this, there is an old episode of a TV show called Magnum PI where Magnum had supposedly died and gone to heaven. So Magnum goes up to his buddy, Mack, in heaven and says, 'Alright man, you know all the answers, so where do we go? How do we get there? What do we do?' Mack stops and says, 'What makes people think that when we die we get this diploma in universal knowledge?' You don't. You are still learning at that place. It would be extremely boring to me if I died and let's say I love apple pie. So it was heaven and apple pie. And every time I wanted apple pie, I had it all the time. In a week, I'd get really tired of apple pie. I believe we go through levels, we go through different dimensions, and we get to learn things. That's it, that's the wonderful part of it, we just don't have a body at that particular time to weigh us down, make us feel sick, and everything else."

5
Inside Jokes

Some of the best reconnections can happen when you least expect it. A lot of times we receive messages personally; however, because we are not taught in our society that this is possible, we may overlook them. When you haven't sought out a psychic medium for the purpose of connecting with a loved one who has passed, receiving this information can be a wonderful and unexpected surprise.

After being married to someone for over fifty years, you are bound to have inside jokes that only the two of you share. Wanda Gausepohl and her husband, known as Bus, had one that even her granddaughter, Melissa McConnell, never knew about.

Melissa has been a close friend of Ricky's for years. She had numerous readings from him and she was always amazed at the accuracy of his predictions. Melissa is blessed to be part of a family that is open-minded. After sharing some of her experiences with them about Ricky, her family invited him over to give readings to some of her family and friends. Her grandmother, Wanda, was in attendance and she met Ricky for the first time.

With the recent media coverage and television shows demonstrating communication with those who have died, Wanda was interested in mediums and their abilities. She was aware of the stories that Melissa had shared regarding Ricky's typical psychic readings and the accuracy of his information, but she did not know the extent of his abilities. This was the first time she'd ever had a reading. When it was her turn, she walked upstairs with Ricky interested but without expectation. She probably wouldn't have sought out Ricky or any psychic for a reading, but since he was there she thought she'd try it and see what he had to say.

Ricky began to give her a typical reading using his angel cards for guidance. After a few minutes, he stopped looking at the cards and focused on the information that was being communicated to him from someone trying to come through. He said, "I keep getting a name that sounds kind of like Buzz or something close to that?"

"Well, my husband's name was Bus," Wanda replied.

"Yes, it's him," Ricky said as he received confirmation from the visitor. He continued, "He's telling me the pants don't fit, the pants still don't fit? Does that mean anything to you?" Ricky asked.

"Yes," Wanda said while smiling, laughing, and

crying at the same time. "It was a joke that he and I shared since the beginning of our marriage. No one knows about it." She knew unequivocally that Bus was talking to her through Ricky. She was filled with joy remembering the many years that they had together.

Bus and Wanda were not only married, they were best friends. They did everything together. They traveled, played cards, went to the racetrack and spent time at their beach house with family and friends. He was a loving and giving man who always found time to help others.

Her husband was not finished verifying his presence, so Ricky continued. "I'm getting something about Saint Seton or Sister Seton. I'm not sure what that's about but he seems to be saying just that, like you'll know what he means. Does that make sense, Wanda?" he asked.

"Yes Ricky, it all makes sense," she answered smiling.

"One last thing, he wants me to tell you to keep on dancing," Ricky said with a smile.

"Thank you Ricky," Wanda said with misty eyes as she reveled in the peace that surrounded her. She loved to dance and she realized that he wanted her to continue enjoying her life in spite of his absence. Her heart swelled with love for her husband and his messages. He'd passed away nine years ago and although she knew she'd see him again one day, when it was her time to go, she didn't expect to hear from him today. What a wonderful surprise she thought to herself.

After the reading was finished, Wanda rejoined her granddaughter, Melissa, and the rest of her family downstairs. "How was it, Grandma?" Melissa and the rest of her family asked curiously. Wanda had a peaceful glow about her as she began retelling them what happened.

"Bus came through to say hi to me," she said through a teary-eyed smile. She told them Ricky had referred to a joke of theirs that they shared. No one knew what it was.

She proceeded to tell them the story. Bus needed a suit for a funeral. Their son David worked at a clothing store as a teenager and he anxiously offered to fit him for it. Reluctant because of his inexperience, Bus declined, but David was relentless so he eventually agreed. Bus and his friend, who also needed a suit for an upcoming conference, went to the store to have David measure them.

As he dressed for the funeral, Wanda watched in dismay as her husband pulled on the pants. They were about five inches too short and he was unable to zipper them. Bus regretted having let his son do the measurements as Wanda said, "That's not your suit, the pants don't fit." They found out shortly after, that David had measured them correctly. He had been given his friend's suit and his was at the conference.

This incident became a joke between them throughout the rest of their marriage. Every time Bus bought new pants, he would joke with her and say, "They still don't fit. The pants still don't fit Wanda!" Melissa and her family were enthralled with the story, not only because it was nice to hear a joke that the couple shared, but also equally as surprised that Ricky had told her that information. There was no doubt that Bus had spoken through him.

Wanda proceeded to share with them the other information that Ricky had given her in regards to Saint Seton. Again, Melissa and the other guests were amazed. Wanda and Bus had thirteen children. When their daughter, Susan, was born she was frail and obviously very sick. The doctor told them she had a cardiac problem and may not live through the night. If she did survive, she would be a sickly child with a lot of problems. They were devastated. That evening, Bus and Wanda along with a priest and nuns, prayed fervently on their rosaries to Mother Seton for a miracle. They asked her to help Susan be healthy. At that time she was referred to as Mother Seton because to become a saint there had to be documentation of a miracle from prayers to her.

The next morning, Susan was stronger and she was able to go home, but there was still a concern over her future health. A couple of years later, the doctors were amazed to see how healthy and vibrant this little girl was as she ran around happily. This was obviously an important and astounding reinforcement of faith in their lives. Melissa and the other guests were in awe of the touching story.

Bus had made a clear and undisputable visit to Wanda that day. His reference to the "pants don't fit" joke emphasized his sense of humor that had lasted beyond his physical death here on earth. Wanda was happy that her husband was able to enjoy the memories they created through their many years together.

She had not expected to have a visit from him that day; however, she was grateful that she had the opportunity to hear from him. She was not shocked or taken aback by the messages Ricky passed on to her. She believed in her heart that Bus' spirit still existed after his death; therefore, she did not need verification that he was ok. Wanda looked at it as an unexpected surprise. It did, however, make her realize that she could ask for her own signs from her loved ones that had passed. She put this to the test shortly after meeting Ricky.

Wanda's daughter Debbie was born with some disabilities. Back then, there was a lack of knowledge and services available to help those who were challenged. Debbie was given a plethora of medications that were believed to possibly have been the reason for her premature death in her late thirties. Wanda had always felt protective of her and wanted to make sure she was doing ok.

Prior to leaving for a trip, Wanda asked Debbie to give her a sign that she was all right. When she reached her destination and opened her suitcase, she found her answer. Debbie had always loved dimes and throughout her life she collected them.

On the top of Wanda's clothes sat a single dime.

The loss of a best friend, a partner, and a spouse of many years can leave you with a void. Bus died at ninety-two, so although they lived a long and happy life together, Wanda missed him and the time that they shared. His reconnection with her was his way of letting her know that he was still around and that he had taken his love and memories with him. It helped reinforce Wanda's own personal belief that spirits do continue to live after death.

Here is what Wanda said to Ricky after her reading:

"Thank you, you are very special and my grand-daughter is lucky to have you in her life."

Here is what Melissa has to say about her and her family's experiences with Ricky:

"For over ten years I've gotten to know Ricky and to this day I am utterly amazed by him and his "gift." He is part of my family and I must say my family adores him, especially my grand-mother Wanda. I am so proud of Ricky and I am truly lucky and happy to say that he is my best friend."

Melissa McConnell

Bus & Wanda Gausepohl

Bus & Wanda Gausepohl

Q & A with Ricky

Wanda was not shocked to hear from Bus because she already believed in the continued existence of spirits. Previously you stated that you believe that a person's "belief system" prior to death is a big determining factor in what they experience after death. Do you feel a person's belief system has any bearing on their ability to communicate after physical death?

"Well to be really more specific, the belief system that the person has before they die is their belief system about 'heaven and hell.' I don't know that their 'belief system' has anything to do with whether they will communicate or not. Once they're on the other side, you know, everybody wants the opportunity to say hi to everybody. Imagine that there is a big wall and there only a couple of glass doors that people can go through. So, everybody tries to crowd around the glass door to get through."

So are you the "glass door?"

"Yeah, I'm the glass door. Sometimes you have to use Windex on me. (Chuckle) In the case of Bus and Wanda, there is such an attachment that you can tell. I didn't know what I was saying to her, but I just said it. It was really clear to her though it didn't make sense to me at different times. But really to answer your question, it doesn't have a whole lot to do with how they'll communicate. For example, if they were a born again Christian and they don't believe in psychics, it may come through in the session that they are saying, 'I was a born again Christian and I didn't believe in psychics' and usually we get a big laugh out of that."

How is it that there is such a clear concise message like "the pants don't fit," a joke they shared for so long throughout their marriage? Is that just like hearing "Bob loved hamburgers?"

"Uh-huh. In other words, they had a very close connection and Bus was a strong personality and they had a strong connection. (What kind of name is Bus for a person? It's like I'll name you truck.) You have to remember too that if little Grandma comes through, she'll be quiet and talk very soft; because that's the way she was when she lived. But Bus definitely was an energy that was Bing, Bang, Boom."

So it was easy to communicate with him?

"It was easy for me to understand."

After Wanda saw you, she asked on her own to hear from her daughter Debbie, who had passed. She asked Debbie to give her a sign to let her know she was around, and she found the dime on top of her clothes in her suitcase. What is your opinion, or do you have a theory on how it is possible that the dime appeared? I mean, it is a physical thing. Can spirits affect the physical world?

"Clearly it looks like they can. I mean, I don't know. It's funny that just today a woman asked me,

"Could my mother's spirit be inhabiting a blue jay that comes to visit me?" And I kind of laughed and said, "Clearly I can hear your mom and your dad has passed too hasn't he?" She answered, "Yes, he has."

"Well he's saying that a blue jay isn't big enough to contain your mom either physically or vocally." But I do believe that they can somehow enhance a sign. If a blue jay was a sign for a person (it meant something) and it makes them think about it, they may have a hand in it. I don't think they jump into the blue jay or anything, but I really wouldn't know. My theory is that they can send signs."

So how did the dime appear in the suitcase at that time and place?

"How would I know?" (Chuckle)

I don't know. I just thought you would have a theory!

"Here I'll make up a name. We'll call it 'meta-physical particle dissimilation.' So there you go."

OK. Next, there are people like Wanda who have a deep religious belief in the continued existence of spirits after physical death. She, and many like her, are not threatened by psychic mediums and do not perceive or judge them as being evil people. However, some people see the work you do as evil or the work of Satan. Why do you think that they are threatened by you and the work that you do?

"Well, the same reason that some people are threatened by members of the Democratic Party. They aren't evil, but some people are threatened by them. Umm, listen, I don't know why people believe the way they do. I really don't. You would be surprised how many people that are born again, Catholic, or whatever, come to see me. It is their own personal belief system that they have going on. You know, all through history people have been afraid of things they don't understand, and some people have actually been intrigued by things they didn't understand. So it is going to be either camp."

If you had a chance to say something to someone who was in front of you who said, " I think what you do is evil and the work of Satan and you shouldn't be doing it," what would you say to them?

"I could say a variety of things at that point. If they came up to me and said, 'I think what you do is evil.' I would go, "Well, I think what you are doing right now is evil. You walked up to me without even knowing me and told me what I do is evil and I didn't ask anything."

Let's put it this way, if someone is reading this book and they are on the fence because they've been taught by their religion that what you do is evil, but yet they feel in their gut that they want to better understand it, what would you say to them?

"I would say that everything comes from either fear or love. If you really feel good about it, it makes your heart swell, and it brings joy to you, I don't think God would be angry at all. But if I'm sitting there saying to you 'If you give me a thousand extra dollars and I put a hamburger underneath your pillow, you'll be able to go to heaven on Thursday,' well there is something abusive about that. Everyone has their own intuition and they should be able to use it. 'Now, why are you asking me these types of questions?'"

Why do you think it is that people are scared or nervous of having a session with you?

"That's pretty simple, not that the question is stupid. But come on, it's the unknown. I mean if someone said, 'Listen, we are going to go skydiving and it is fun and we do it all the time.' When your ass gets to the edge of the plane and it is time to jump off, you might be petrified! You know, I think it's normal to have some apprehension. Some people are very excited, they are dare devils, and they do it."

What would you say to someone who was scared to come see you? Maybe they really want to, but they are scared because they think it might be wrong, or they may be scared to know when they are going to die or whatever."

"Usually I don't tell someone when they are going to die. The couple of times that happened with me, the person already knew they were going to die. If you are scared, it is natural to be apprehensive, but there is no reason to force yourself to do it. If you don't feel like you are ready, don't."

6

Daddy's Little Girl

Expectations that one has going into a medium session can sometimes lead to disappointment. The loved one that you most want to hear from may not always come through. However, keeping an open mind when it comes to the messages that you do receive can be important for you or someone you know. It may take persistence to find out why things happen the way they do.

Greta Reimann heard about psychic medium, Ricky Wood, from her hairdresser. She told her that during her reading, a friend of hers who recently passed away had come through. She was amazed at the details that he'd given her. Greta had been to psychics before, but she'd never been overly impressed with what they had to say. She became excited thinking about the possibility of hearing from her father who had passed away a few years ago. Greta was always daddy's girl and she missed him terribly. She decided to have a party and see what Ricky had to say to her.

As the day approached, Greta was full of excitement hoping to hear from her dad. They were very close. She was a tomboy growing up and they played and attended a lot of sports events together. Earnest Reimann was very protective of his daughter especially when it came to men in her life. He instilled the belief in her that she should always be independent and self-sufficient so that she would choose a man for all of the right reasons. He wanted her to find her own happiness and success. What he didn't want was for her to rely on a man emotionally or financially and set herself up for devastation if it didn't work out.

When it was her turn for a reading, Greta was a little nervous. For the most part, she was full of anticipation to hear from her father or her grandmother whom she was also very close to. Ricky began by telling her that the room was full of women. An older relative named Margaret was the main person speaking. Greta was somewhat confused.

She hadn't felt particularly close to her great Aunt Margaret while she was growing up. Ricky told her that she was the one who was in charge of planning her graduation party, which helped Greta determine who was speaking to her. This was her way of letting Greta know that she showed her love through actions more so than words. She also told her how proud of her she was and how much she loved her. Ricky then told her that her aunt had a message for Greta's mom. She said, "Tell her I said hello, and to prove to her that it is me, tell her about the dresses." Greta had no idea what that meant, but she made a mental note to tell her mom after the party.

Greta's reading was coming to an end and she felt somewhat disappointed. She asked Ricky if any men wanted to speak to her. He told her that there were men there, but the women were very strong and they wouldn't let the men through. Although Greta was somewhat dismayed, she laughed because she did come from a family of very strong-willed women.

After the party, Greta spoke with her mother. She told her that Aunt Margaret had said hello and to prove it to you that it was her she said, "Tell her about the dresses." "What does that mean Mom?" Greta asked confused. Her mom told her a story from her childhood that Greta had never heard before.

As a little girl, she'd struggled with weight issues. Her mother would always buy her dresses that were too small for her. They were then given to her sister, who was thinner, to wear. Her Aunt Margaret would make her a matching dress in a size that fit her. This was another example of how she showed her love and affection through taking action. This was something that had always touched her heart and she was grateful for the message.

Greta realized how much her great aunt had loved them both. This made it apparent to her that people show their love in different ways and she felt newfound warmth in her heart for her great aunt's kind deeds. After hearing her mom's childhood story, she was even more convinced of the authenticity of Ricky's reading. This made her even more curious about other messages she would get in the future. She still had a longing to reconnect with her dad. She was letdown after having a second session with Ricky and once again not hearing anything from him. Although he gave her undisputable details and she found it helpful and enlightening, she didn't understand why she hadn't heard from her dad.

Earnest had always expected a lot from Greta, probably hoping that she would set her standards high for herself. When she was twenty-nine, he passed away. Unbeknownst to her at that time, Greta would struggle with choosing men that she was drawn to verses what she thought would make her dad proud. She worked hard to obtain her own financial success and she purchased her own home. Relationships with men, however, remained on the backburner in her life.

Greta shared the experiences she'd had through Ricky with numerous family and friends. She had enough requests to have another party, so she invited Ricky back. She wasn't sure who she'd hear from this time, but she hadn't given up hope that her dad would come through. However, not wanting to feel disappointed, Greta didn't expect to hear from him or anyone in particular.

When Greta sat down across from Ricky, she

couldn't help but feel at ease. His casual and friendly demeanor seemed to have that effect on her. As he began, she noticed that his body immediately changed. He sat up very straight and proud in his chair. The inflection in his voice even seemed to change as he said, "Your dad's here Greta." Her heart began to race with excitement. She thought it seemed odd that Ricky's mannerisms had changed and they were now reflective of her dad. He continued, "He's telling me he finally trusts me enough to come through. He didn't think I was the real deal but now he does, so he's here," Ricky said seeming almost surprised at what he was saying. Greta's heart was beating wildly with anticipation. He was finally here she thought knowing it was just like him to make sure that Ricky was authentic before coming through!

Ricky continued, "He's showing me a German Flag. He's very proud of his heritage." Greta laughed as she remembered her family attending the German club picnics as a child. She recalled seeing the German flag that he had hanging in his office at work. "Your father wants you to be more proud of the German part of you," Ricky said almost verbatim as her dad had said to her so many times when she was growing up.

"Yeah, that's something he would say," Greta responded with a smile. She thought of his hat covered with pins from Germany that she had hanging on the coat rack in her foyer. It brought her comfort to see it every time she came home.

Earnest worked hard to provide for his family. He spent many long hours at the office; however, every minute he wasn't working, he spent with his children. "He wants you to know that he wishes he could have been there more for you," Ricky continued on with Earnest's message to his daughter. Greta felt a lump rising in her throat as she saw flashes of her childhood. She missed him so much she thought as she refocused her attention on what Ricky was saying.

"He is so proud of you Greta. He says you exceeded every wish he had for you. Now he wants you to find someone to share your life with," Ricky stated soothingly. Greta felt as if her dad was there, telling her all the things she wished she'd hear from him. She could no longer fight her emotions, and with a heave the floodgates opened cascading her heartache down her cheeks. Her whole body tingled as she marveled in her father's love that seemed to be enveloping her. She had promised him the day that he had died that she would make him proud. It seemed almost as if he was lifting the weights from her shoulders freeing her from her infinite expectations.

As Greta brushed some of the tears from her cheeks Ricky went on. "Your dad is saying that he knows that you're interested in a man of a different race, and he wants you to know that he's completely ok with that. He says he doesn't see color anymore, only the character of the person. The only thing that is important to him is whether they love, respect, and treat you well." Greta's eyes filled with a pool of fresh tears. She'd always thought that her dad's dream for her was a tall, blond hair, blue-eyed German man. She no longer felt like she had to find someone to fit the mold she thought he wanted.

As her reading ended, Greta felt like she could fly. For the first time since his death she realized that what her dad wanted most was for her to look inside herself and realize what made her tick. He wanted her to fulfill her dreams. From that day forward, Greta felt free to follow her heart knowing that honoring herself was the greatest gift she could give him.

Her reunion with her dad has changed her outlook on life by giving her the freedom to manifest her own hopes and dreams. She is truly grateful that she was able to hear from him through Ricky. She still talks to her dad every night knowing definitively that he hears her and loves her as much as he always did. Although Greta still misses her dad being here with her physically, she finds great comfort knowing that he's not gone.

Here is what Greta has to say about her experiences with Ricky:

"Ricky Wood has always been a source of positive energy in my life. Every session I have had with Ricky has left me with an optimistic outlook and motivation to achieve my aspirations in life. Ricky's ability to connect with my loved ones that have passed never ceases to amaze me. Ricky has been able to speak with my father discussing family secrets that no one else could have possibly known. Ricky is a very talented life coach and psychic medium. I recommend Ricky to all of my friends and family."

Greta Reimann

Greta dancing with her Daddy.

Earnest Reimann

Q & A with Ricky

In this story, although Greta wanted to hear from her father during her first session with you she did not until her third. Mr. Riemann said through you that he needed to trust you first. This sounds like something a human who is living and can't see the 'bigger' picture would say. Can one still have trust issues even after crossing?

"It is my belief that when you die, lets say you loved chocolate, well your body goes away but you still like chocolate. You know that doesn't all inherently go away. You don't get like a diploma in all-knowingness on how to act."

Wouldn't that go away because it is a physical aspect?

"It is actually a spiritual aspect also."

Craving chocolate is a spiritual aspect?

"Yeah."

I guess I do agree with that!

"What I'm saying is, think about it this way. If they didn't feel some of those things on the other side, and it's not like they are like WHERE'S MY CHOCOLATE, it's just more like if they lost every aspect of their humanness or who they were as a personality, we'd all be out of business. Because they would be like, everything is ok, welcome, how are you, things are good. That wouldn't have been anybody that Greta would have recognized. In other words, they make it so the other person can understand who they are, because I have no idea why I would have said to Greta that it took him a while to trust me. But that's what I felt and that made perfect sense to her. Whether or not he really doesn't trust, I think it was to let her know that it was part of his personality. If he has said, 'I trust this guy, he's wonderful,' Greta would have been like, 'you've got to be kidding me, my father didn't trust a man on the planet.'"

Mr. Reimann was able to "see" that the color of one's skin or their ethnicity did not have anything to do with who a person was. So I guess I'm confused why after crossing over he was able to see beyond skin color, yet he still had "trust" issues that came through you. Is it that after crossing you may "get" some things and not others?

"I don't know. But here's the deal, like I said before, if he had come across all trusting, Greta would not have understood that. But if he came across a little non-trusting, like he had been with her on the physical plane, then she could identify with that. They try to get people to identify."

So it may not be that he didn't think you were the one to talk to his daughter, it was just part of the personality he was conveying and the message he wanted her to get was that it didn't matter who she dated regardless of his skin color as long as she was happy and he was good to her.

"Yes, in death you no longer have a body, so imagine being around a whole group of energies with no physical characteristics. They're all just beings of light. You could greet Tyrone, Wong Fu, Jack, or Luigi—the only thing is the names. To them there is uselessness in that."

What are some of the other reasons that you think or believe that a spirit does not come through?

"I think it depends on a couple of things, it could be the condition of the medium—how tired or energetic that medium is, or the spirit's energy level. Remember, if they are whispering or really quiet, it may be harder to do. Also, I believe it sometimes depends on whatever is for your highest good. The highest message at that time really should be the medium's job to give. Sometimes, the world, heaven, God, the universe or whatever you want to call it has three great answers. Yes. No. Wait. Sometimes it's not the right time. Sometimes it's yes, hey, come through. Other times it is no, and there could be a variety of reasons why. Maybe that person has grown too dependent on the medium. There have been times when I've had to tell people, 'You were just here three weeks ago, and there's no reason for you to be back here having a mediumship session to find out what the dead want you to do. The dead want you to live life and learn all the lessons involved in it.'"

What would you say to a person who really wants and needs to hear from a specific relative who hasn't come through yet? Would you say to get another session? Wait? Or what? Like Greta really wanted to hear from her father. She came to see you, left time in between her sessions, and waited but she didn't give up because she needed to hear from her father.

"I would say you have a couple choices. You can try it again, or try and find another medium. For whatever reason, maybe another medium is the one. If the time is right, it'll happen. And usually ninety percent of the time, the time is right."

7

Nana's Love Really is Forever

There is always a special person in one's life that is the most influential. Their belief in you, their strong shining example, and their unwavering love helps shape you into who you are. Your gratitude is shown when you share your successes with them. Unfortunately, these may not come until they have passed on, leaving you with a sadness and longing for their presence at your most memorable events.

Stacey Carlitz was having her hair done in her friend Tina's salon when she met Ricky Wood. At that time, he was still in the supplement retail business and he had recently opened a store two doors down from the salon. Tina told Stacey that he was a psychic medium and she should go and get a reading from him. Stacey had the day off so she figured she'd go and see what he had to say.

In her late teens she had been to a very good psychic who'd impressed her; therefore, she had a belief in psychic abilities. She had not had an opportunity to visit a medium before so although she was intrigued, she wasn't sure about their authenticity. If spirit communication was a reality, she really wanted to hear from her nana, her maternal great-grandmother Elizabeth D. Ingram.

Stacey was twenty and a junior in college when nana died. She did not have much of a relationship with any of her grandparents, so her nana was all of them rolled into one, as well as a second mother figure. She learned from her to be a strong, self-sufficient woman who fulfilled her own dreams and chose to share her life with a man. Nana taught her that she didn't need a man to take care of her. She also engrained in Stacey to always give to others and to be kind and generous. She often said that whatever you do in life would always come back to you.

Stacey checked her blond hair in the mirror, thanked Tina, and headed out the door towards Ricky's store. She looked down and realized that she was in sweats, and she wasn't wearing any jewelry except for one ring that she had reset to include a stone from one of her nana's rings. She wondered if she would finally be able to hear from her.

Stacey longed to hear from her nana as she recalled all the times she wished she were still alive to share in her triumphs in life. Nana had always been her greatest teacher and her inspiration and she was saddened that she hadn't been there to be a part of her special occasions.

As she sat down in one of the two chairs on either side of the small table, she smelled a whiff of incense. Ricky sat down across from her as he adjusted his baseball hat. He began, "Do you have a piece of jewelry I can hold?"

"Yes, here," Stacey said as she slipped the ring off of her finger and handed it to him.

"Shuffle these," Ricky instructed as he handed her a deck of angel cards. When she finished, he began to lay them out. He abruptly stopped as a strange look covered his face. He turned the cards face down and said, "I don't need these." Stacey was taken aback and wondered why he was saying that.

"A woman is coming through who is short in size, but she has got a lot to say," Ricky stated matter-of-factly. "She won't let anybody else through and she's bombarding me," he said appearing overwhelmed. "Wait, wait, you've got to slow down so I can get all the information through," Ricky said appearing to be talking to someone in the room she couldn't see. As he refocused on Stacey's blue eyes, he continued, "She is someone from your mother's side of the family and for some reason she wants me to sit like this," he said inquisitively as he sat up straight moving his shoulders back and pushing his chest out.

Stacey started laughing realizing it was her nana as she recalled what she'd thought she had heard her say a thousand times as a child, "A woman should always sit with her shoulders back or you'll be round shouldered. Bust out, shoulders back!" Ricky continued by putting his pointer finger in the air and saying, "You weren't meant to be like this. You better cut it out and start eating right." Stacey sat up straight and felt as though her Nana was speaking to her directly. "Do you know what that means?" Ricky said sternly.

"Oh, Yes," she replied feeling as if the world had just came to a standstill. She was floored realizing that her nana was still very much around.

"When you visited her, which you did very often, would you park in an alley in the back of the house where there were steps that creaked as you walked up them?" Ricky asked.

"Yes," Stacey responded as she recalled entering her nana's house.

"I see drawings, little kid drawings hanging on the wall, all the way up the steps." Stacey smiled as she remembered how her nana had hung up every picture she'd made at her house.

"Are you a writer for a newspaper?" Ricky asked cocking his head to the side.

"No," Stacey said a little confused.

"Well, she's showing me a newspaper and another newspaper, and another. I see her taking them out of a drawer," he said scratching his head.

A smile covered Stacey's face as she replied, "Well, I used to write for the Pit News in college, and I sent her the newspapers," she explained.

Suddenly, she remembered that when her nana had passed away they had found her newspapers in the drawer next to her bed. She had saved every single one. Chills covered Stacey's body recalling that day that she had forgotten about. "She is so proud of you," Ricky exclaimed as his eyes shined with pride. A warmth encompassed her body as she realized that she had shut out a lot of the memories of the days and weeks that followed her nana's death. "She wants you to remember your creative side and get back to it," he said soothingly. "You've forgotten that side of yourself."

Ricky quickly continued feeling a sense of urgency to get out all of the information he was being given. "Why haven't you had children yet? You're married aren't you?" Ricky asked although he seemed to already know the answer.

"Yes, I'm married. I haven't had any children yet for a lot of reasons," Stacey replied realizing that she wasn't wearing her wedding ring.

"Well, you are meant to have a child, and your nana wants you to know that there is a soul waiting for you and that you need to have a child," Ricky said. "I don't usually say this, but you are meant to have a child that will better mankind," he stated. "She wants you to know that you can't deprive the world of this soul that is waiting for you and that you need to get on with it," Ricky said adamantly.

Stacey felt like her head was spinning. She had been contemplating a child and she felt as if she was being given the chance to discuss it with her nana, the single most important and influential person in her life. Stacey didn't have many odd moments in her life, but she was having one now. Embracing the scientific side of her mind, she rarely felt as if things didn't make logical sense. It was as if a boulder had dropped out of the sky and landed in front of her on the table.

"She's laughing and showing me this little plastic kit, like one that a doctor would carry," Ricky said with a questioning look. Stacey could no longer hold in her emotion. Her chest heaved and she began to bawl. Tears began streaming down her face as if carrying away the barricades she built when her nana passed. "Are you ok?" Ricky asked concerned.

"Yes," she said as she wiped some of the tears from her cheeks. "My family tells me this story all of the time. My nana used to take me to Kiddie City when I was little. One time, when I was eight, I decided I wanted a doctor's kit. She was short and couldn't reach them up on the wall so she asked a man to get it down for her. He pulled down the white nurse's kit and she said 'NO! My Stacey is going to be a doctor when she grows up. She wants the doctor kit, the black one.'"

Ricky continued, "I can only tell you what I see. Sometimes it doesn't make sense to me, but maybe it will make sense to you. You stayed at her home a lot?" he asked.

"Yeah, every weekend," Stacey said with a smile.

"You had a room in her house. She's showing me a room with a little plaque on the door that said Dr. Stacey or doctor something, and when you opened the door there is a desk with paper and stuff in it?" he said questioningly.

"Yeah, that was my office," Stacey said joyfully remembering the years she had spent there.

"What do you mean your office?" Ricky asked confused.

"That was my office. I would spend hours in there playing doctor and writing prescriptions. I always knew I would be a doctor. There was never a question that I would be anything else when I grew up!" Stacey said jubilantly. "I am a doctor," Stacey said as fresh tears moistened her eyes.

Nana wasn't finished with her messages, so Ricky continued on. "I'm seeing you standing next to your husband. You are wearing a wedding dress and your husband has a tux on. You are looking at a piece of artwork in a frame that has writing that I can't read on it. It's not English. It's nothing I'm familiar with," Ricky said as he asked her to explain what he was seeing.

"I'm Jewish," Stacey said recalling her wedding day knowing that her blond hair and blue eyes weren't typical attributes of people of Jewish decent. "Before you walk down the isle to have your ceremony, you have a pre-ceremony with the immediate family where you sign your marriage contract, which is called a Kettubah. It is created by an artist and it is written in Hebrew," Stacey continued explaining the Jewish marriage tradition. "The man and wife see each other prior to the traditional ceremony to sign the contract and to make sure that the groom is getting who he is supposed to be marrying versus waiting for the veil to come off at the end of the ceremony."

"Your nana says that she was standing right behind you saying 'I'll sign, I'll sign,' and 'what took you so long?'" Ricky said with a smile. The Kettubah is only signed by men and Stacey laughed knowing that her nana's ahead-of-her-time personality was saying that it didn't matter if you were a woman; she would sign it for her!

As Stacey recalled her wedding day, she remembered having felt a deep sadness that her nana wasn't there to celebrate with her. Realizing that in fact she had been there was a dream come true. Stacey was so overcome with emotion that she was having a hard time catching her breath. She felt as if her whole world was opening up and releasing the grief of not having her nana present at her most important events -- from her graduation from college and medical school, and her wedding.

The Earth seemed to be moving rapidly under her feet. As a physician, she had fully embraced the scientific philosophy of logic that a + b = c. She cried as if she was an eight-year-old girl again, wrapped in the loving arms of her nana after so many years of missing her. She recalled the grand feeling of being a child and appreciating the simple joys of home, the smells of food, no worries, and loving the feeling of being loved. All at once the realization hit her that her nana hadn't missed anything. She had been with her for all of her important occasions. Stacey reveled in the bliss of sharing with her nana all that meant so much to her. She no longer felt lonely.

Ricky began speaking again so Stacey tried to refocus on what he was saying. "I want you to take a message back to your mom from your nana. I want you to tell it to her like this, 'Jackie, you're not going anywhere. You've got a long life to live, so cut it out! I know you're dreaming. I know you're thinking about death a lot. I know you're scared. You're not going anywhere, but I want you to know that when you do pass, I'm going to be the one that's going to be there for you. I'll be the first one that you see.'"

Stacey became worried and asked, "Does that mean she is going to die?"

"Well she's going to die someday, but no, this is a message that your mother needs to hear," Ricky explained. Stacey was confused because she had no idea why she was supposed to say that to her mother, but she agreed to pass it on.

At the end of the reading, Stacey stood up trying to steady her self and all of the emotions she was feeling.

"Wait, I have one more message," Ricky said. "The picture. There's a picture. You know which one. You use to have it in your dorm, next to your bed in medical school, and it hasn't been up. What is it?"

"That is my favorite picture of me sitting on my

nana's lap holding a telephone," Stacey said with a smile.

"She wants the picture hung, you need to hang it up," Ricky said.

Shortly after the reading, Stacey gave her mother the message. She was amazed when her mom told her that she had been dreaming about death, and thinking about Stacey and her sister when they were little. She had also been crying a lot while looking at their baby pictures. Stacey's mom was blown away that nana was aware of that and she heeded her message to get back in the world with her children now.

After the initial shock of the whole experience subsided, Stacey was able to digest all of the information that she was given. She realized that her nana was telling her that she needed more balance in her life. As proud of her as she was for all that she had accomplished in her career, she wanted Stacey to remember and embrace her creative and spiritual sides.

It has been four years since Dr. Stacey Carlitz met Ricky for the first time. During this time she has rediscovered many parts of herself that she had neglected for so long. Her reunion with her nana has changed her life and opened her eyes to viewing the world in a whole new way. She feels a completeness embracing science along with all of the multi-faceted parts that make up who we are. Knowing that her nana is not gone gives Stacey a profound joy that has changed her life.

Here is what Stacey has to say about her experiences with Ricky:

"Thank you Ricky from the very bottom of my heart, a place seldom seen, for helping me to see the need to restore the balance in my life that I have for so long been missing. No longer do I solely define myself by my life's work as a physician, but more importantly as a woman, a wife, a daughter, a friend.

Thank you Nana, for always managing to find a way to guide me through life's journey. In death as in life, you will always be the wind beneath my wings. You are the first face that I see when I awake each morning and the last thing that I see before I close my eyes to go to sleep."

Stacey Carlitz

Stacey watching her husband signing the Kettubah on their wedding day.

*Stacey's favorite picture of sitting on Nana's lap
while on the telephone.
(The one Nana wanted her to hang up)*

Elizabeth D. Ingram

Q & A with Ricky

In this story, you told Stacey's Nana to "slow down so I can get all the information through." In your experience, do the spirits understand what you are saying to them? For example, you've said that it isn't always easy to understand what the spirits are trying to "say" to you. Do you feel that they have any problems understanding you?

"I'm sure they do."

So when you say, "Slow down," do they?

"It slowed down somewhat. Some energies are stronger than others. They are clear and fast. Others are slower."

From your experience, do they generally respond to your requests?

"I don't really request a lot of them." (Chuckle)

I mean when you don't get something and you say "show me something else" or "slow down," or whatever.

"In other words, I don't always go 'SHOW ME SOMETHING ELSE!' What happens is, if I don't get it, I wait until I get something else."

Oh, well why?

"Why not? I mean, I can only relay what I get."

So you don't feel like it is a two way street where you can ask for something?

"Some people I'm working with I feel like they'll even try to clarify. All spirits are not the same."

Overall then, do you think it is easier for spirits to understand you than it is for you to understand them?

"I think it may be a little easier for them to understand me."

Is that because they don't have a body to impede it?

"I have no idea."

Stacey had been overwhelmed at the realization that her Nana had in fact been present during her important life events. Here we talked about her wedding day. Do you think it is typical that family members that have passed are present during these events?

"I would probably have to say be careful of the word 'typical.' I would think that if they care and they love, then they send their loving energy to those events. I wouldn't say they get in their spirit car and drive on down to the wedding. I'm just saying that they would be there. They love, you feel them. If someone's father or mother has passed, there is a tendency to feel them or feel their love. It kind of infuses them with all of the love and happiness that is at that event."

Stacey's Nana mentioned her wedding day and stuff like that, you know the major events that

Stacey had been wishing her Nana could attend. Do you think our loved ones' spirits are only present during special occasions?

"Listen, Bobby Smith's annual poker game could be the biggest thing to somebody. I would say that they are always going to be there for you with love and understanding. When you are sitting on the toilet, it may not be the most loving and understanding moment in your life, but they'd be right there if you need them. Um, for Stacey with her Nana, it was important for Stacey to have her Nana there, and she would have never let Stacey down."

I know a lot of people who spend some of their "special days" feeling sad or wishing that someone who has passed was present. What advice would you give to people who are sad when a loved one can't be physically present during a special day? How could they open themselves up to know or feel their loved one is there? Is there a practical tool to even see or notice a sign?

"I don't know if there is a 'practical tool,' but I would tell you this. If it was someone's father and they were very close to that child and that child was walking down the isle one day, I can guarantee you that their energy will be there. They wouldn't miss it for the world. Just like in life they would say, 'I wouldn't miss it for the world.' You know if someone is in Iraq and they can't be with their child on their birthday, I guarantee you that daddy or mommy is with them on that day no matter what. You are just thinking about the human body being there. Intent is an incredible thing. So, don't worry. And sometimes Uncle Bob will be there and you might not want him there. But he may be there too."

Some "scientific minded" people may find it hard to believe in spirit communication. Here Dr. Stacey was given irrefutable proof which opened her mind to all that science cannot explain. What would you say to the argument that psychic mediums are "not real" or "hocus-pocus" because there is not scientific proof behind it?

"They are entitled to their opinion. Period. They don't have to believe and it isn't my job to convince them. I think positive energy is much better than negative energy anytime. You know if they don't want to believe, they don't have to believe. But the truth is if someone is feeling it, and it touches their heart, the heart is a great way to get in touch with what you have going on. Try it sometime. Close your eyes, ask yourself a question, and put your hand over your heart. You'd be surprised at what you get. I'm not really concerned with the people that don't believe. That's like trying to get people who love nothing but NASCAR to go see world soccer matches, it just doesn't happen."

Except maybe when it just out-of-the-blue happens like it did with Stacey, maybe then they'll believe – you know?

(Shrug)

Ok, I'm just excited and want everyone to be able to experience it, but never mind let's move on. Would you compare intuition, spirit communication, and such with the "unseen" science such as gravity, electromagnetic fields, or quantum physics?

"Uh-huh, yeah."

So a "scientific minded" person could relate to what you do in those forms?

"Using your words, there have been many 'scientific minded' people who have come to see me. It is their particular belief system that allows them to 'get it' or not. In other words, I don't know how electricity works. I'm completely befuddled by the fact that a TV can show me a show. A box that has a plug in it will show me a TV show, the news... It is just amazing to me that someone could invent that. But I'll watch it, I'll enjoy it, I'll even change the channels. I don't really need to know how it works."

8

Still Shaking

If you are blessed with having one true friend in this lifetime, you are lucky. Not just a casual acquaintance or someone that you hang out with once in a while, but an individual that truly touches your soul. They make you a better person for having known them, even if it is only for a short while.

Carla Falcone is one of those lucky enough to have experienced such a friendship. From Tim Callari, she learned that there are people who are trustworthy and kind. He gave her an inside view of a lifestyle that she did not truly understand. Unconditional love and non-judgmental acceptance were two of the many intangible gifts she received from him. Although she only had seven years with him here on Earth, their friendship lives on. Four years after his passing, they met again.

Carla walked into her friend Gerri's kitchen to say hello to everyone at the party. Ricky was there to give readings. He had just finished one and was getting himself a drink. Carla still had her coat on when Ricky turned to her with a funny smile and said, "I want to see you next." As the other women at the party began complaining that they had been waiting, Carla became a little freaked out. It wasn't that she was scared to get a reading-- she had been to psychics many times before, but she was taken aback by Ricky's urgency to see her next. Carla had been to a psychic that had called herself a "medium" before and she had not been impressed. Hoping that Ricky wasn't going to tell her something bad, she followed him upstairs.

Carla took off her coat and sat down. Ricky sat across from her and asked, "Do you have a piece of jewelry that I can hold?" She slipped her amethyst ring off of her finger and handed it to him. He held it for a moment and said, "I'm getting a strong vibration from this and I feel like it is in two parts, like it wasn't always this way. Does that make sense to you?"

"Yes," Carla responded as she smiled remembering Tim giving it to her for her twenty-first birthday. She had since had the ring reset a little differently in white gold instead of the original yellow gold setting.

"The person who gave you this loves you very, very much but he wasn't a boyfriend. It wasn't a sexual relationship," Ricky stated. "Oh, here he comes again," Ricky said with a smile referring to the person he had heard come through in the kitchen. "Ok, I guess I'm just going to have to do it,"

Ricky said as Carla stared at him inquisitively. She wondered just where he was going with this and what he was talking about.

Ricky proceeded by shifting his body to the side of the chair and cocking his legs to the left in an effeminate manor. Then he raised his hand and proceeded to shake only his first finger. Instantaneously, Carla felt like she was sitting across from her friend Tim. She drew in a deep breath, stunned by the very specific mannerisms that Ricky portrayed. They weren't the typical depictions of a gay man. He didn't cross his legs or use his hands a lot. He only shook his first finger from side to side just like Tim. Tim had died four years ago, but she could swear he was sitting across from her! Chills covered her body and then quickly dissipated as she was overcome with anticipation to hear what he had to say.

Ricky picked up his deck of angels cards to use; however, he quickly placed them back on the table and said, "Everything I need to know about you this guy is going to tell me. He's not going to let me use them; he wants to talk to you. I feel tightness in the chest. It's not cancer, it is some type of blood disorder, and he was very, very tired," Ricky said. He asked, "Do you know who this is and what I'm talking about?"

"Yes, my good friend Tim died from AIDS," Carla replied although she had already known it was him from the mannerisms that Ricky had been using.

"He is acknowledging your breakup with your

boyfriend. He's saying it's about time. It took you long enough! You know he wasn't good for you!"

Carla smiled and said, "I know" feeling like she was hearing it directly from Tim's mouth. After going back and forth for the last couple of years, she had finally broken off an unhealthy eight-year relationship. She smiled knowing that Tim would be happy about it and thinking how nice it was to hear him say it.

Ricky began to shake his finger back and forth as if saying no, no, no, and he's saying, "The girl with the diamond ring, the really big ring, don't trust her." Carla was amazed. She had heard this before from Tim years earlier when they all worked together at a salon. He had always told her not to trust or get too close to this particular girl who was known for having the huge diamond ring. Recently, Carla had begun to hang out with her a little more. She laughed, as she thought about how much Tim hadn't liked her then and obviously still didn't!

"Who is Lucinda?" Ricky asked.

"I don't know a Lucinda," Carla replied confused.

"Well, he's doing the whole thing. I'm seeing him in a dress and he's saying Lucinda," Ricky said smiling. Suddenly, it hit her.

"Oh my gosh, that was the name he used when he got dressed up as a girl!" she said. "Every Halloween and when he entered gay beauty pageants, he would dress up! That was one of the names he used!" Carla said laughing as she reminisced about the fun times they had.

Ricky replied laughing, "I guess I should have known that he meant himself."

"He also wants you to know that the reason you don't have a boyfriend isn't because of the way you look," Ricky continued, "You need to knock it off! You will find someone who will love you just the way you are, just the shape you are, and just the size you are," Ricky said soothingly. "You have to stop thinking about the exterior because that's not what is important," Ricky said matter-of-factly. Carla smiled as she thought about how she had been overdoing it at the gym recently. She was working out like a fiend, and she knew that she was going past maintaining a healthy lifestyle with it. Carla felt as if she was having a conversation with Tim again and it felt great.

Warm feelings enveloped her body as she stood at the end of the reading. She was enjoying her reunion with her dearly missed friend, and she wished it didn't have to end. Carla was elated as she rejoined the party to share her incredible story. She was so happy that she had a chance to chat with Tim once again. Although Carla was surprised by his visit, she was not saddened or completely shocked.

Raised as a Catholic, she always had the belief that the spirit did not die with the body. Since his death, Carla had numerous dreams and feelings at times that he was still around. She would wake up while dreaming that he was sitting on the end of her bed talking to her, and for a split second she could swear he was still there. Other times the dreams would resemble the old times when they were laughing and joking at work.

Although she missed his physical presence, Carla seemed to innately know that he watched over her. Tim treated her as a younger sister while he was alive, and she felt that it had not ended with his death. He taught her so much about the acceptance of others regardless of the way they looked or what their sexual orientation was. Carla was given the opportunity to ask him questions about what homosexual relationships were like. She found that they were no different than heterosexual couples in the respect that they ultimately sought unconditional love and happiness.

Tim's straightforward and honest approach to life was a shining example to Carla in her young adult life. His genuineness and ability to make her laugh is something that she will never forget about him. Thankful that she had the opportunity to know him, even for a short while, Carla will forever carry Tim in her heart.

She is grateful that she had the opportunity to talk to her friend again. Although she believed that Tim's spirit lived on even after his physical death, her session with Ricky helped to further reinforce it. She also gained more confidence to trust herself when she felt like Tim's spirit was visiting her.

Here is what Carla has to say about her experiences with Ricky:

"My experience with Ricky was very special. To have a friend as special as Tim was wonderful and to speak to him again years after his death is amazing! Ricky truly has a gift and he uses it to promote health, happiness and healing."

Carla Falcone

Tim dressed as "Lucinda" for a beauty pageant.

Carla & Tim

Timothy Joseph Callari

Q & A with Ricky

In the beginning of this story, Carla had not even taken her coat off at the party when you told her you wanted to see her next. How are you directed to a specific person at a party? Is it like when you look at them you hear something said to you or is it like magnetic? How do you know that is who you are supposed to see next?

"It's weird. I mean, when I saw Carla it would be weird. People would be saying they wanted to go next, and I would say no I feel like you ought to."

So it isn't like you heard someone say something?

"Like words 'TAKE HER NEXT,' no I felt it though. Feelings are a good guide for me. That's all."

One of the great things about this story was you shaking your one finger which was exactly what Tim did when he spoke. Did you get an overwhelming urge to sit that way and shake your finger or were you seeing him and you were imitating him because that is what he wanted you to do? How did you know to shake your one finger and put your legs to the side?

"Sometimes I don't realize I'm doing that. I don't even know that this is coming out that way. I just did it. I didn't hear him or see him do it, it was just a feeling that I went with and did."

*Is it like the feeling we get in the pit of our stom-
ach when we just know something, or what kind of
feeling are you talking about?*

"All that I know is that I'm feeling it, so I do it.
It would be like Aunt Lucille always used to scratch
her armpit, you know and I would feel like scratching my armpit. I'll go, 'I don't know why, but I feel
like I'm supposed to be scratching my armpit.'"

*So it is like an overwhelming urge or feeling to do
that thing?*

"Yeah."

*When someone comes through and you do this
mimicking of the thing the spirit used to do as a
physical being, is this kind of like channeling –
when a spirit comes into your body and acts or
speaks through you? Is it a form of that? Kind of
like the movie "Ghost"?*

"I have channeled before and that is a different
feeling. Channeling is when a spirit comes through
a human host to speak. It may be a small form of
that, but usually when I channel it is an ascended
master or a teacher guide speaking through me."

*In some of the stories we heard about you using
angel cards. Sometimes you begin to use them, but
then put them down because the spirit was talking
and you didn't need to use them. Can you explain
what "angel cards" are?*

"Well, fifteen or so odd years ago, a woman
named Gail, who was a friend of mine, knew

that I kind of liked this stuff, but I had just started kind of doing it. She told me she thought I should have them. So she gave me these Angel Oracle Cards."

What exactly are Angel Cards? Are they like Tarot Cards?

"No they aren't like Tarot Cards. They are cards that have beautiful pictures of Angels on the back of the card and the other side may have a word like happiness or death. They don't have specific meanings for each card. Well if they do, I didn't get them with directions that gave specific meanings for each card, so I use my own interpretation. I use the cards as landing points which means when I'm doing a reading, they help me use my intuition more. That's all."

So when a spirit comes through really clear in a medium session you don't even need the cards?

"I would say during most medium sessions when people are coming to my office, I don't use cards a whole lot. They are more for psychic readings and to help at parties."

Tim and Carla seem to still have such a love and closeness with each other that physical death couldn't destroy. Do you think that some friendships like this connect spirits through death and rebirth?

"I don't think the human body has anything to do with being friends. They could have been friends for many lifetimes. People have soul groups. I believe they attract people over and over again."

What are soul groups?

"Soul groups are groups of souls that get together and decide what kind of work they are going to do. You know, people to assist you. Who is going to be the mother, the father, who is going to be the one to cause problems. You will always have certain people that you connect with. I believe that it is people that have always connected with you, whether it is in this lifetime or other lifetimes. We have a tendency, I believe, to search out those people again. Sometimes I think the bigger strength comes from the ones who have to be the 'bad' guys for whatever lesson needs to be learned."

9

I Will Remember You

Experiencing a traumatic loss as a teenager can have a life altering impact that can cloud the rest of our lives. Healing can be greatly inhibited without an understanding of the continuation of one's spiritual life after a physical death. Although we may be taught that our spirits live on, it may be hard to grasp without help. We will never forget the person we lost. When met with irrefutable evidence that they still exist, true healing may begin.

Before she began college, Erin Grieco had no idea how much her life would change. One summer evening, her best friend Jennifer McGehean called and asked her to come over. Upon arriving, Erin was told that Jenn had driven a friend home and that she would be back shortly. After waiting for what seemed like forever, Erin decided to go home and get some sleep because she was very tired. As she drove away, she looked back over her shoulder hoping to see Jenn pulling into her driveway. She couldn't shake the eerie feeling in the pit of her stomach that something was wrong.

In the middle of the night, Erin dreamt that her phone was ringing but she couldn't get to it in time and the caller hung up. When she finally reached it, she pushed *69 and recognized Jenn's phone number. The next morning she received a call, and the uneasiness she had felt was confirmed. Jenn and her friend had been in a car accident. The skid marks showed that her brakes had locked while swerving to miss something, which caused her to collide with a tree. One of the branches had made its way through her head down into her chest. She died instantly.

For the next seven years, Erin struggled with the loss of Jenn. Bouts of depression and tears regularly plagued her for she could not deal with the void that encompassed her. She missed Jenn's smile, laughter, classiness, and most of all her true friendship. Having known her since the sixth grade, Erin felt as if she lost the sister she never had. She treasured the lessons of self-acceptance and self-love that Jenn had taught her. Erin longed to speak with her beloved friend one last time.

During a visit to Pennsylvania to see her family, Erin heard about Ricky. Her aunt had been to see him and she was amazed by his abilities. Erin decided to call him and see if she could make an appointment. When he answered, she introduced herself and said, "I'd like to make an appointment. I'm not going to be here for long."

"I'm sorry," Ricky responded with a dry humor. Erin began laughing hysterically as Ricky joined her.

"No, I mean I'm not going to be in the Pennsylvania area long," Erin said, still laughing. She was happy that he had an opening for an appointment that afternoon. Erin hung up the phone, still smiling at Ricky's quick wit.

She desperately wanted to hear from her friend Jenn. All the way to his office, she looked up at the sky and said, "Geez Jenn, I really hope this is going to work. I really hope I get to talk to you, Jenn!" Before entering Ricky's office, she put on her serious businesswoman you-won't-get-one-over-on-me face because although her aunt had raved about Ricky's authenticity, she still had reservations.

Upon entering his office, Erin said, "Well, I don't know if I want a whole hour session. So if I want to stop at a half an hour because if it's not making sense then..."

"Don't worry, girlfriend. I'll tell you what you want to know. It's not going to be your way or the highway. Don't worry, you'll get what you pay for," Ricky said, chuckling.

Erin smiled and thought to herself, "Wow, he shut me up!" She sat down and placed her favorite picture of Jenn and herself on the table between them. Jenn's mother had given it to her. It was the one that used to sit on Jenn's dresser in her bedroom.

Ricky picked it up and looked at it for a moment. "Is she a really bubbly, nice girl?" he asked. Still filled with apprehension and not wanting to give him too much to work from, Erin responded shortly, "Yeah."

"Well, she is just hugging and kissing me, she is so happy you are here," he said smiling.

Ricky began rubbing his chest as he said, "I'm seeing a lot of blood, blood in the lungs." He then quickly touched his head and made a sweeping motion from his head down to his chest. "I see blood on her shirt, a lot of blood," Ricky said while making a circular motion with his hand around the center of his chest. Erin's body froze as she recalled the heart wrenching details of how Jenn died in her car accident. She shook the gruesome image from her head and the statement she had heard that Jenn had lost almost all of her blood very quickly. It was far from the beautiful, free-spirited girl that Erin remembered.

"Ok, so why is she showing me a puppy?" Ricky asked. Her forehead wrinkled, as she had no idea what he was talking about. "Puppy, puppy, she keeps saying," Ricky said adamantly. "Puppy? I don't know, because she loved cats," Erin said confused.

"Ok, now she is saying May 21st. Why is she saying May 21st?" Ricky continued. Suddenly something clicked in Erin but she didn't want to let him know, she wanted him to continue, so flatly she responded, "Ok, what else?"

"She's saying the puppy and May 21st, you

know what she is talking about," Ricky continued interpreting.

"Yeah, that is the date I got my puppy, Cassidy, a couple of years ago," Erin said unwilling to give up any other information.

"She's saying something about the eyes, she's showing me the puppy's eyes," Ricky said. Erin's body began to tingle and her distrust and skepticism began to recede. From the moment she met her dog Cassidy, she felt as though they could communicate with each other through their eyes. It seemed that Cassidy knew what she was feeling and vice versa just by looking at each other. Although she wouldn't have believed it had it not happened to her, she swore that she had a special bond with her dog that was far from typical.

"Jenn is saying that Cassidy is really playful," Ricky said.

"Yeah," Erin responded, trying to fight the feelings of calmness and knowing that were enveloping her.

"Jenn comes to visit you sometimes through Cassidy and she sent that dog your way because you needed her at that time," Ricky said soothingly. Although she wouldn't say so to him, Erin felt an understanding that she'd never felt before. It all made sense. Two years ago she had moved from Pennsylvania to Montana with her boyfriend and she didn't know anyone else. The first summer there, she bought Cassidy. It had been a huge move and although she was happy to be with her boyfriend, at the time she had felt somewhat alone being so far away from her family and friends.

Ricky began speaking again and Erin tried to refocus on what he was saying. "Why is Jenn wearing a Bob Marley shirt?"

She smiled as she responded "Jenn's mom let me have her favorite Bob Marley t-shirt after she died."

"Well she's wearing it, she's happy and laughing," Ricky said through a smile. Chills covered Erin's entire body and she felt a peacefulness radiating through her. She knew Jenn was present talking to her through Ricky and she wanted to hear more.

"Does she miss me, Ricky?" Erin asked feeling a lot more comfortable.

"No, silly they don't need to miss you, they have that luxury," Ricky said lightly.

"Well, does she know how much I miss her?" Erin asked, her voice filled with sentiment.

"Yeah, she does and she's saying if you'd quit staring up at the sky and talking to her and shut up long enough to listen, you would realize she's either playing a song for you, or she's sitting right next to you," Ricky said. "Pay more attention to the radio and different signs, she is trying to come through to you." Erin's head was racing. She tried to breathe and calm down so she could concentrate on what Ricky was saying.

"You have a lot of souls around you, Erin," Ricky continued.

"I do?" Erin inquired skeptically.

"Yeah, Jenn was there at *your* accident." Although she felt like her heart was beating so loudly that you could hear it throughout the room, Erin played it off again as she did not want to feed him any additional information.

"Yeah." Erin responded flatly.

"Jenn's saying that you got messed up!" Ricky said.

"Jenn was there?" Erin asked.

"Yes, a bunch of others too or else you would have lost that arm of yours," he said as he brought his hand down on his other arm in a chopping motion. Erin's head was racing as she looked down at her arm that was not visible through her long sleeves. A huge scar covered it all the way up and around her elbow. She recalled her mom telling her that immediately upon coming out of her coma, that Erin had told her that she had seen Jenn. Erin had lost all her doubts about Ricky's authenticity as she looked back up at him. "They didn't want your loud, talkative mouth over there yet so they sent you back!" Ricky said smiling.

"Yeah, I believe that," she said laughing at the accurate depiction of her personality.

"She is making me feel like she's still not done yet," Ricky said still referring to Jenn.

"Oh, yeah," Erin said with a content smile.

"Why is she showing me a bar here in West Chester? She's not from this area?" Ricky asked inquisitively. Erin immediately knew what Jenn was referring to.

"After she died, I went with her mom two or three times a year to the bar and restaurant in town to talk about Jenn," Erin said with misty eyes.

"I'm meeting a friend after I'm finished tonight. Come back at eight o'clock, we'll go there. She wants you to go there. We'll toast to her," Ricky said feeling that this was important to Jenn. This would be the first time that Erin toasted Jenn's life and continued existence instead of mourning her loss.

Erin knew her session was coming to an end and she wanted to know if there was anyone else there that wanted to speak to her. Her cousin had died tragically and she didn't know if she'd come through. "Is there anyone else who wants to say anything?" Erin asked.

"There are a lot of souls around, but the whole ride over here you kept saying Jenn, Jenn, Jenn, I want to hear from you," Ricky said sarcastically. She smiled realizing that everything he had said to her in the last hour was a hundred percent accurate. Feeling as though she was floating, Erin left his office.

After putting her parents' concerns to rest about going out with strangers, she returned to the waiting room in Ricky's office a few minutes before eight. His door was closed because he was with a client. One other woman was sitting alone reading a book. Erin didn't notice if there was any music playing until suddenly, as if someone had turned the volume all the way up, she heard the words from "I Will Remember You," by Sara McLachlan.

As the song continued to play, Erin felt her body begin to shake. It was the song that she and her friends played and dedicated to Jenn. Looking over at the woman reading, she realized that the volume obviously wasn't as loud as it was inside her head. Overcome with emotion and not wanting to cry in front of someone, Erin ran to the bathroom. When she regained her composure she returned to her seat in the waiting room.

Shortly afterwards, Ricky emerged from his office and approached Erin. He put both of his hands out as if he was saying, "See, I told you. She's standing here in a sundress and bare feet and holding her hands out to say see, you just have to listen," Ricky said smiling.

"I know the radio… and her song…" she said unable to form a complete sentence realizing that she hadn't told Ricky about Jenn's song.

Chiding her Ricky said, "She's saying you just about cried!" Stunned that she had recognized a message on her own, Erin was speechless.

Although Erin was raised with the belief that spirits still existed after one's physical death, she had a hard time believing this until experiencing it first hand. There are no longer any doubts in her mind. In hindsight, Erin wishes that she was able to listen to her messages from Ricky without such skepticism and distrust; however, reconnecting with Jenn meant so much to her that she wanted to make sure that Ricky was the "real deal." No longer filled with doubt, she is looking forward to getting another reading from him.

Erin still struggles with slowing down and really listening to messages that are being given to her directly. Knowing that she is able to do this without help, she continues to try to find ways to welcome them on her own. Since her session, Erin looks at Jenn's physical death in a whole new way. Although she continues to miss her physical presence, she no longer cries when thinking of Jenn because she knows that she isn't gone.

Here is what Erin has to say about her experience with Ricky:

"I had been dealing with the sudden death of my best friend Jenn since 1997 and still was when I met Ricky in 2003. I was sent to Ricky through a family friend who had an amazing session with him. I went in with all guards up and feeling a little apprehensive about our meeting. Ricky instantly called me on my bluff and had me settled within minutes. The things that Ricky told me about Jenn, me, and my past were things that no person would know without knowing me. His humor, compassion, and overall attitude made me feel as though I was talking to a best friend. All guards were down and a sense of calm was their replacement.

I soon became a regular client by having Ricky as my "Life Coach" through phone conversations from my home in Montana to his

in Pennsylvania. Ricky was able to guide me through my pain and insecurities all awhile using his amazing abilities to keep in touch with Jenn. After years of laughter filled conversations and amazing transitions in my life, Ricky is still an amazing friend. I have found an inner peace with my loss and have learned so much about myself and the decisions I make. His guiding, caring, and uplifting attitude makes him an addictive friend that holds a very special place in my heart. I see Ricky every time I come back to PA and I cannot ever see myself letting go of such a special and meaningful friendship!"
Erin Grieco

Erin & Jenn

Jennifer Lynn McGehean

Q & A with Ricky

*Experiencing a tragic loss can have a huge im-
pact especially on young people who haven't yet
found their own footing in a belief system. A lot of
us have been taught that you die and then go to
heaven, which seems a million miles away. What
would you say to young people who are trying to
cope with the loss of a friend or family member
and they feel like that they are just gone?*

"Heaven is in Montana -- ask Erin. (Grin) I
would say that as corny as this may sound, if you
search your heart you'll always have connections to
those people that you love. You just will, especially
if there is a strong bond between the two of you."

*What advice would you give to parents about ex-
plaining physical death and teaching the existence
of the spirit?*

"To a really young kid, I would say, 'Death is a
lot like being alive, just without a body.'"

*So how do you explain where the spirit goes?
Would you say that it walks around among us, instead of the typical going-to-heaven-up-in-the-sky
story?*

"First I would say you get reunited with the people that you love the most. Grandparents, cousins,
and friends who have died before you will be there
waiting for you. That is what I would tell a little
one."

What would you tell a teenager when they can grasp more details?

"I would tell a teenager that what is on the other side would basically be the same. The people you love and care for will be there to greet you and to look for them."

But what if they wanted more detail. If they asked what happens when you die, would you say "you go up into heaven where it is all fluffy, beautiful, and peaceful"?

"I would say the experience is individual. It would depend on their religion and their belief system. I really believe that one's belief system really carries a lot of weight when it comes to going to heaven. In other words, I've told you in previous chapters that if someone is Muslim and Jesus Christ was there to greet them, it would be a bit confusing. So I believe there would be other Muslims there to greet them."

So what would you personally tell your teenager based on your belief?

"I would tell my teenager that for me that there would be people who have passed before me there to greet me."

But what is there?

"I don't know."

Typically when someone dies, we hear, "They are at peace now. They are in heaven where it is beau-

tiful. They don't hurt anymore." Do you think these are statements just to appease us so we can be relaxed and think that they aren't in pain and are better off? Where does this come from?

"Well, I believe that our bodies carry a lot of physical pain, so imagine if you had not one iota of physical pain. None. It doesn't mean, though, that there isn't an emotional consideration. I'm just saying that without a body, there isn't a whole lot of pain. But, all learning doesn't stop. I believe that you continue to learn and there are opportunities for souls that are there."

Why is heaven made to seem like it is Hawaii or something. Is it beautiful and peaceful, and whatnot?

"How should I know what it looks like? I'm not there yet."

Well, don't you get glimpses or someone tells you?

"No."

Can't you ask them?

"They say it looks like Hawaii. But the ones who have never been to Hawaii say it looks like Cleveland."

Well I believe that it looks like Hawaii even though I haven't been there yet.

"But Hawaii still has bugs."

Well then it is Hawaii with no bugs. So what do you believe?

"I believe it is a state of feeling. It is a vibration. I know you are trying to get concrete answers for people, but as a living person who hasn't been there or can't remember..."

My twelve-year-old daughter Cassandra interrupts and asks, "What she is asking is, Are spirits still here? Is someone sitting right here next to me or am I sitting on them? Where are you? Are you up in the sky, are you down here, are you down in the ground, where are you?

"The worms crawl in, the worms crawl out, the worms play pinochle on your scalp. (Big laugh by all) To tell you the truth, I believe that it is all vibrational. What I mean by that is spirits exist on a different plane. Think of it this way. In order to catch up to the speed of a humming bird, you would have get wings and beat those wings just as fast that humming bird so that you could catch up to it. Imagine spirits moving really fast like that -- like a blur. That is their vibration to me. We are here. We can feel this couch we're sitting on, and all that. There, it is different. What I can say is that it feels like love. As dumb as that may sound, it feels like love. It is a happy place. A place of understanding, and if love could be a place, then that is what heaven could be."

In this story, you said that Jenn sometimes visits

Erin through her dog Cassidy.

"I will say this before anyone gets the belief that somehow Cassidy has been inhabited by Jenn. No. I believe more that Cassidy is a sign or symbol for Jenn. We always get signs. I'll never forget when I lived in Landenberg, Pennsylvania. For three days in a row at the same time, a big tom turkey landed on our deck. You would hear this big thud, and it would just stand there. I really don't know if it was my dad. I doubt it. I don't know who it was. It could have just been a turkey. Maybe it wanted me to get my rifle. Just kidding, I don't hunt."

So when you said to Erin that sometimes Jenn visits you through Cassidy. What does that mean?

"I don't believe that it means the dog is inhabited by Jenn. However, I do believe that Jenn uses Cassidy as a sign."

When Erin asked you if Jenn missed her, you told her, "No silly, they don't need to miss you. They have that luxury." Is that because they don't miss us because they still "see" us?

"Yeah, also I think time is just a drop in the bucket. This lifetime is a drop in the bucket and they get that. Erin doesn't have to worry about Jenn because Jenn knows that one day Erin will join her. For Jenn, it will be like seeing her next Tuesday."

When you knew it was important for Erin to go to the bar and toast to Jenn's life for the first time instead of mourning her loss, it seemed easier be-

cause Erin was given proof that Jenn still existed. However, it can seem really hard for those who have not received information like this. How do you suggest people celebrate a loved one's life instead of mourning it? Maybe get a medium session? What else can you do?

"I think sometimes when you speak to a medium, it gives you validation from another point of view, which can make it easier. The other thing you can do is always celebrate their lives by celebrating your own. As corny as that may sound, that is the best way to honor it. You know, Erin came to see me because she wasn't feeling that connection. I know Erin needed to know more. Looking up at the sky and talking wasn't enough for her."

That isn't really enough for anyone is it?

"Yes, some people are ok with people dying and they will never ever need to see a medium. They are fine with their faith, and know that they are in a good place and it will be ok."

Do you think that happens more when their loved one died from old age or they knew it was coming? Is it harder to be "ok" with it when death was a tragic or unexpected loss and the person was young?

"When someone has been yanked from your life, you know, it's hard. And that is what happened to Erin. Jenn was yanked from her life. Here's something else. There are a lot of people who come to see me through the weirdest ways. They happen to be at the right place at the right time. So and so came to see me and bumped into so and so, who bumped into so and so. Erin was all the way in Montana, but came back to Pennsylvania to visit her mother. So the spirits sometimes do a little nudging themselves. How they do that you might ask? Well, I really don't know."

10

A Mother's Love Never Dies

There is no one like your mother. For most of us, she is the first and most important person in our lives. The safest and most content place in the world is in her loving arms. Most mothers would agree that it is the hardest yet most fulfilling job there is. It is beautiful to see those moms who have the uncanny ability to make every day with their children count.

Growing up, Shawn Detterline wanted for nothing. His mother, Rosanne, spoiled him and his younger brother. She was the type of woman who relished being a mom. Rosanne did not sit back and watch her sons play in the sandbox; she was in there with them. Her children were her world and their wants and needs came before anything else. If her kids were happy, she was happy. Shawn gladly embraced the fact that he was a "mama's boy."

He fondly recalls the simple times that brought him so much joy. It didn't matter what they were doing as long as they were together. One of his fondest memories was their ritual of walking into town, renting a movie, and getting Chinese food. Just being with her on the couch was the happiest place on Earth for him.

Shawn smiled as he looked around at the party he was at with his mom. His heart swelled as he saw her laughing and having a great time. Contently watching her, Shawn noticed that his mom looked happy and the most beautiful he'd ever seen her. From a distance, he heard his fiancée's voice and felt her touching his arm. Shawn fought to stay in the moment, but as he awoke, the image of his vibrant mother faded.

Reality set in. She wasn't there with him. It was about a year after her death, yet the dream felt so real. He was left comforted knowing that she was ok. Innately, Shawn knew that his mom was trying to tell him that she was happy and that she wanted him to think of her that way instead of dwelling on the memories he had of her suffering. He still gets choked up thinking about his inability to take away her pain during the end of her life.

Rosanne was diagnosed with Leukemia in her late forties. It was a long and painful battle that she fought for years. She was tenacious and did not give in easily. Shawn, at twenty-six, was working and attending college. One evening between work and school, he stopped in the hospital to visit her as he often did. She was sleeping at the time, so he went over to the side of her bed and said, "Mom." She opened her eyes and Shawn said, "I love you."

Rosanne smiled at her son. He watched her eyes close as he left the room.

The next morning he received the phone call that his mom had passed on. As he listened to the words that he knew would come, tears covered his face. There was no way to prepare himself for the devastation and helplessness that he felt. Trying to find some comfort, he thought back to the last time he saw her alive. He was grateful that he had been able to say goodbye to her.

With the help of family, friends, and his fiancée, Shawn found the resolve to move on after his mother's death. Although it was extremely difficult without her, he found it easier when thinking of ways to make her proud. Shawn did well until his relationship ended with his fiancée. She had been such an integral part of his life during the sickness and passing of his mom. The ending of the relationship devastated him. He lost the stability that carried him through the most difficult period of his life. One evening when he felt very alone, he lay in his bed thinking of how much he missed his mom. From the stillness came what felt like a hug from her. He knew his mom was there with him, then and always. There was no doubt in his mind that she watched over him.

Shawn's Aunt Monica had been to see Ricky numerous times and she had heard from Rosanne and other deceased relatives. She knew that if Shawn saw Ricky, he would probably hear from his mother. A friend was having a party and Ricky was going to be there, so she asked Shawn if he wanted to go. He was excited and agreed immediately. Although he already knew that his mom's spirit was around him, he looked forward to hearing what she had to say.

About an hour before seeing Ricky, Shawn began feeling a little nervous. He was confident that his mom would come through; however, he knew there was no guarantee. When it was his turn to follow Ricky upstairs, his anxiety grew. Within moments of sitting across from Ricky, he felt a peacefulness surround him as Ricky began to speak.

"How long has your mom been gone?" Ricky asked.

"Approximately three years," Shawn responded as he watched Ricky intently.

"Well, she's saying she wants to smack you upside your head," Ricky said lightly. Shawn laughed at the statement that he could easily see his mom saying. Ricky elaborated, "What are you doing? You are not doing as well as you used to because you are using her death as an excuse, kind of like you are in a self-destruct mode."

Shawn looked down as he thought about the last eight months of his life. The messy breakup with his fiancée had caused him to go into a state of despair. Losing her was even more devastating because she had been with him through his mother's death and helped him during his mourning process. He was lonely and depressed because his rock was gone, and he fell prey to unhealthy behaviors.

Shawn rubbed his chest to ease the dull pain that radiated from it. "I've been trying to do better recently, reading a lot, and trying to heal and find peace," Shawn said as he looked at Ricky, but seemed to be speaking to his mom.

"She knows, stop beating yourself up," Ricky said soothingly. "Your ex would have done this to anyone; it wasn't you or something you did. You are going to meet someone kind that will have your back. You will be very surprised when it happens, but it will." Shawn felt a wave of relief covering him. Having her acknowledge his pain with his ex and assure him that everything would be ok made him feel as though his mom was sitting there with him.

"She wants you to forgive her Shawn," Ricky said soothingly. "For leaving you early and she wants you to forgive yourself. There was nothing you could have done." Shawn had held his emotions together for most of the reunion, but he was unable to do so any longer. The lump in his throat became too large and he let go. Tears freely fell as he basked in the surreal moment. It felt almost as if he was a little boy again and his mom was hugging him with a protective and loving hug that only she could give him.

"I can forgive her. I don't blame her for leaving early. I just need to forgive myself because I love her so much that I feel guilty that I couldn't do something to help her, especially when she was suffering. I miss her so much," he said with a pained look on his face. As Shawn wiped away the tears he continued, "I don't want her to see me upset or crying."

"You can't be happy all the time. She's going to see you upset and that is ok," Ricky responded.

"Do you like the Eagles, the football team?" Ricky asked as he cocked his head to the side.

"Yeah," Shawn responded.

"Well, she is showing me a stuffed animal bird with an Eagle's shirt on it," Ricky said.

"I have always loved the Eagles" Shawn responded smiling at his mom's reference to his favorite football team.

"There is also an older man with your mom -- your grandfather, I think. He is smoking," Ricky said.

"That is probably my pop-pop," Shawn responded smiling as he recalled a picture of him when he was alive in his mind.

Ricky continued, "Well, he's saying be tough! That's it, just be tough."

"Sounds like him," Shawn said amused at the short and sweet manly advice.

As Shawn's reading ended, he was overcome with emotions. He was elated that his mom had come through to talk with him. Although he already knew she was around him, hearing words instead of just feeling her made it seem more real. He cried for having lost such a wonderful mother, for the pain she had to endure at the end, and the void he felt without her physical presence. The final tears were filled with joy because he knew she was happy and that she had never really left. He knew that her physical body may no longer be here but that her spirit is still very much alive.

Shawn is truly grateful that he had the opportunity to hear from his mom again. Although he already knew her spirit was around him, hearing the words reinforced his belief. Since his session with Ricky, he has had additional dreams in which his mother was present. Each one helps the memory of her last years of suffering fade a little more. He finds great comfort from them because she is happy. Shawn knows unequivocally that his mother's love never died.

Here is what Shawn has to say about his experience with Ricky:

"I have always been an open-minded person, so I was happy to talk to Ricky about my mother and the things I went through earlier that year. It is very hard for anyone who loses a parent. I would like to thank Ricky for providing the opportunity for mom to comfort me again. Hearing the words made me feel better, and I know she's always watching over me. I love you, mom."

Shawn Detterline

Roseanne Detterline

Rosanne Celeste Detterline

Q & A with Ricky

In general, it seems that women are more open to psychic readings and they come to you much more often than men. Why do you think that is?

"I think that women are more in touch with their feelings. Women are more open-minded but more men are becoming more open-minded and in touch with their feelings everyday."

Do you think it was easy for Shawn to come see you because he already believed or was more open to it because of that void and wanting to connect with his mom?

"I don't know because I'm not Shawn. He had that feeling and only he can say why."

Well in this story it is clear that Shawn had a strong connection with his mother, he already felt her presence and dreamed of her often, yet he was still suffering because not only did he miss her physical presence, he couldn't let go of the suffering that his mother endured before her physical death. This seems to be one of people's greatest fears – the physical pain felt before death. Even if you believe in an after-life, you may fear that moment before death when you have to feel that excruciating pain.

"Well I don't know if it is always excruciating."

But I think that physical pain is a fear for most people, maybe even more than what the after-life holds.

"Yeah, I think for some people they may have a fear of dying, physical pain, and the unknown."

In this story, Shawn told you that he was upset with himself because he couldn't stop the physical suffering his mom had to endure at the end. This seemed to be impeding his moving on because, although he knew his mom's presence was still around him, he was finding it hard to let go of his inability to stop her pain before her physical death. What are your thoughts on this?

"Well, when you love someone, you wouldn't want them to suffer. You would want to do something to help ease that suffering."

Do you think for some of us that "letting go" of suffering seems like we are disrespecting our loved ones. Almost as if the pain, sadness, and not letting go equal loyalty and the continuance of loving them? That maybe letting go of the pain is letting go of the love we had for them.

"I think what you are trying to say is, 'If I am not suffering then I'm not thinking about them.' That is not true. Wouldn't it be wonderful to think about them with joy? I do think that everybody has to go through their own individual mourning process. But once you have gone through that, a great way to honor them is to celebrate their lives with joy."

But how do you get over the suffering, pain, ending thing? I mean for some people it may be simpler, but for others, like me, it took sixteen years. I don't think that amount of time is really normal.

"Well, it is because people may have other issues going on. For some people, it may take eighteen weeks. For some people, it may take eighteen years, and for some people, they never get over it."

Having been in pain for so many years, and not wishing it on anyone, it is sad to me that some may never get over it.

"That is sad. But if someone was asking me how to do it, I would say to try and celebrate the lives of their deceased loved ones. You know, a lot of people equate them not being here as pain. So, I do think that we have to respect each others' ways of grieving. Some ways may be better."

Do you think that some of the peace that people get from seeing you is that they are able to "let go" of some of their pain from the loss? It seems less like a loss when you realize that their spirits really aren't gone.

"Let's put it this way. If your best friend died and he used to call you 'rutabaga' and no one else knew that nickname and out of the clear blue sky someone is talking and says 'he wants to tell you rutabaga,' well then you **know** there is a connection to that person. When that happens and you get a sense of their personality then you will get that there is something bigger and greater than just living here on Earth or on this plane."

Roseanne told her son, Shawn, through you that she wanted him to forgive her for leaving early and to forgive himself because there was nothing that he could have done. Forgiveness seems to be a huge part of healing. How can we change the way we view physical death? How can we blame less and release feelings that cause unnecessary suffering?

"Well, there are other cultures that do very well with the transference of life to death. They prepare people for what to expect and that type of thing. Western culture has never been that big on that. But I would say this to anyone, there are so many different circumstances. Someone might be feeling bad because they just couldn't handle watching a relative shrivel up, or be sick, or not look good or vibrant. They don't know what to do with that so, sometimes they hide. There are so many different aspects of coping. Not everyone acts the same during the time of death. You know, in some families there is a caretaker who is the 'angel' who takes care of the person—bathes them, feeds them and is there emotionally for them. Some others may love the person, but just can't be there during the dying times. They may be used to 'daddy' being vibrant with a full chest, muscles, and smiles. But to watch someone wither away is a constant reminder of what the dying process of the body is. That is scary to a lot of people."

Do you think that is because they are unsure of the continued existence?

"No, I think some people know there is continued existence, but the dying aspect is really tough. We don't honor it that much here. If someone has cancer or a debilitating disease and they wither away, it really isn't attractive. The year before, they were 210 pounds of muscle and now they're 130 pounds and can barely move. Now they're a withered husk. It isn't attractive. That is the time when you really need to see the soul. It is hard for some people."

Do you think that the suffering involved with the loss of a loved one is part of the lessons or the things that we need to learn? Couldn't it be easier learning to do it in a way with less suffering?

"I heard once -- and I can't even remember who said -- 'Wouldn't it be great if we could learn our lessons through joy instead of fear.' I think that it is a choice to some degree."

Don't you think that it starts with parents being more open with children in talking about life, spirits, and physical death so that death isn't such a scary, taboo subject?

"I think they should talk about it, but my belief system won't be your belief system. It would be great if there was a 'how to' guide. I wish there was a *Death for Dummies* book (which now someone will write), but you know every child is different, every person is different and every family is different. I think if you do your best to honor that within each family, I think you'll be ok."

11
Danny Boy

Some people believe that when the body dies, so does the spirit. If we are brought up to believe that the spirit survives after physical death, for the most part we are taught that the "good" go to heaven and the "bad" go to hell. What is rarely discussed or debated is what happens when someone's body dies and their spirit doesn't know it. Earthbound spirits have generally been considered a "forbidden" topic. Deanna Dicampli experienced this situation firsthand and now knows that not only do spirits survive their body's physical death, they sometimes remain here instead of crossing over.

From the moment that Deanna met Danny, they became friends. A year later following their first kiss, they were inseparable. Her daughter, Gianna, who was three years old at the time, already knew and loved him. Gianna, who called him Danny Boy, welcomed him into her life with open arms. Over the next two years a happy family gelled and they became engaged and planned to wed. Both mother and daughter were smitten with the always smiling and happy Danny. He loved them both and brought joy to their lives.

Unfortunately, prior to the wedding, Danny was involved in a car accident, and then a work accident when he fell off of a ladder. He was prescribed pharmaceutical drugs to deal with the lingering pain. Before he fully recovered, he was dealt an even bigger blow when his best friend, Joey, died. Unable to cope, he began abusing his prescription drugs to try to numb himself inside and out.

Eventually, realizing that he didn't want to continue down that road, Danny went to rehab. Deanna stood by him, knowing that he was a good and kindhearted man who was in pain, and didn't know how to deal with it. Following a second stint in rehab, Deanna discovered what he learned while he was there. Someone he met told him that he was wasting his money on pills when he could get the same high from heroin for ten dollars a bag.

After postponing the wedding twice, Deanna had to make a decision. She chose to leave Danny, especially for Gianna's sake. Danny was unable to remain drug free and she knew that wasn't the life she wanted for her daughter and herself. Although she physically left, a part of her heart remained. Maintaining their friendship, Danny still checked up on Gianna. As much as he wanted a life with them, he was unable to conquer his demons.

Devastated that she was unable to have the

family she wanted with Danny, Deanna concentrated on giving her daughter the life she deserved. Although she wasn't over him, she remained physically apart from Danny. Their friendship ensued as neither one could see living without each other. Eventually, Deanna became friends with a kind and caring man named Carmen. The two fell in love and married a couple of years later in April of 2005. Deanna was happy that she'd found what she had always wished for. Even still, Danny remained a part of her life.

One year later, in May of 2006, Danny unknowingly obtained a bag of tainted heroin. Upon ingesting it, he immediately met an untimely death. Both Deanna and Gianna were devastated, not only for losing a man that both had loved dearly, but for being unable to say goodbye. Although she wasn't a really religious person, Deanna felt Danny's presence around her. Shortly after his death, a plethora of strange events began to unfold.

At first, the little things brought Deanna comfort. She told Gianna that when you found a penny on the ground that it was a penny from heaven sent by angels. This was a way that those who had died said hello to you when you were sad. After vacuuming one evening and making sure that nothing was on the carpet, Deanna left the room. A minute later she returned to find a penny sitting there right in the middle of the carpet. Once in a while, they'd find one in front of the door and it made them smile.

The signs became more and more apparent as

time went on. On numerous occasions, Deanna would return home from work to find Gianna's picture off the wall and sitting next to the bar in her basement. There was no possible way to get it there without someone moving it. Neither her husband nor Gianna had touched it. After returning it to its place on the wall, it would happen again soon after.

As time went on, even more odd experiences happened. The phone would ring and Deanna would answer it to find no one on the other end. She began checking the caller id to find out who was trying to call. To her amazement, it showed 215-000-0000. Knowing that this was impossible, she would go back to look at it again, and miraculously it was no longer there. Numbers did not disappear, they had to be deleted, yet this happened on five occasions. Deanna also received a phone message which began with a whistle, followed by a strange mechanical sounding voice that said, "Talk to me please." Danny had called Gianna as a toddler by whistling the same way. One day when talking to Danny's sister, Deanna accidentally recorded over the odd message. When she played their conversation back, there was a break in the tape and you could still hear the whistle and "Talk to me please." Then, the conversation between Danny's sister and her continued.

At work one day, Deanna received an email in her inbox. After opening it she realized that it was an email between her and Danny that was written prior to his death. However, it had been modified adding in statements like, "You are the only girl I could spend forever with, but honestly I would die for you." After locating the old email, Deanna compared the new one to it. Sure enough, it had new information in it that was not there before. Deanna knew unequivocally that Danny's presence was around her. Although some of the occurrences were strange and hard to believe, she did find comfort in knowing the he wasn't just gone.

Just prior to the first anniversary of Danny's death, one of Deanna's friends told her about a reading she had with Ricky. She was so impressed with him and his abilities that she was having him do readings at her house. Not having been impressed with psychics before, Deanna reluctantly agreed to go. A week before the party, Deanna's friend had something come up and she was unable to host it. Deanna offered to have it at her house. Suddenly, the once comforting signs she thought she had received from Danny intensified to the point that she was shaken.

Unexplainably the electricity would shut off for no reason. Things began falling off of the walls. She felt anger at her husband and wanted nothing to do with him although he had done nothing wrong. There was knocking at her door when no one was there. One evening that week, Deanna felt her husband trace a heart on her back in bed as he had often done. Afterwards, she felt a D and an S drawn underneath. The next day she asked

Carmen if he had drawn on her back and he told her yes, he'd drawn a heart. When she asked if he'd written anything else, he told her no. Instantly, Deanna knew that it had been Danny who'd added his initials. Also, during the week prior to Ricky's visit, she had a vivid dream in which she saw him. Deanna told him to say goodbye but he refused.

The day of the party she was beside herself. Deanna was overcome by a nervous energy that left her nauseous. When Ricky arrived, his friendly and calming manner put everyone at ease including her skeptical husband and Danny's parents, brother, and two sisters. But for some reason, Deanna wanted nothing to do with him. Ricky's first statement to Deanna while talking to her and Carmen in the kitchen was, "You need to stop being so mean to him. He's a good guy." Deanna tried to look at Ricky, yet she was unable to make eye contact. "You and I are going to talk," Ricky said.

Walking away, Deanna said, "Hem, yeah, whatever." She busied herself and let everyone have their turn with him.

When her time finally came, she found herself again unable to look into his eyes. After some talking Ricky said, "I'm afraid you are not in love with your husband. You don't love him do you?"

"Why do you say that?" Deanna asked, knowing that she indeed loved him but she'd been unable to feel it lately.

"This doesn't make sense. I'm seeing you as a mirrored image, like I'm seeing you as the most beautiful girl in the world. Don't get me wrong, you are attractive, but I don't look at people like that. Why am I here?" Ricky asked confused. "How are you connected? Is he your ex-boyfriend?" Ricky asked trying to look Deanna in the eye as she avoided it.

"The ones you read before are my ex-fiancée's family," Deanna said.

Suddenly, her neck became tight, and she felt like she was freezing, yet she was sweating and clammy. "What is going on?" Deanna asked shaking and unaware of what was wrong with her.

"Danny doesn't want me talking to you," Ricky said.

"Why?" Deanna asked.

"Because he knows I'm here to have him leave. You are going to let him go," Ricky said. "No I'm not," Deanna said.

"You have to let go," Ricky said. Deanna began crying hysterically. She hadn't felt like she wanted to, but it was as if it was beyond her control. She was overwhelmed with the sensation of pulling on the side of her neck.

"He has touched you," Ricky said.

"I know," Deanna answered. Knowing that dealing with Danny's spirit would take all of his energy, Ricky told Deanna he needed to finish the other two readings and come back to her.

While waiting, Deanna nervously kept asking everyone, "Where is memom? She didn't come through? Where is memom?" Danny's family was confused and asked why she cared. Deanna felt an unexplainable anxiousness about memom, which was Danny's grandmother who had already passed.

In between readings, Ricky came up and asked, "What does the Radisson mean to anyone here?"

"That's were Dan and I were suppose to get married," Deanna answered.

When Ricky was ready for Deanna again, she asked to bring some others with her. Reluctantly, he agreed because of how adamant she was. Danny's brother, two sisters, and Deanna's best friend followed her down to Ricky. Deanna's nervousness, stiff neck, and clamminess returned even stronger. She would not look Ricky in the eyes again. "Look me in the eye," Ricky said to her.

"I am," she replied feeling like she was trying to but couldn't.

"Look me in my eyes," Ricky said loudly. As she did, Ricky said, "Dan, you are dead. You died of a heroin overdose."

Ricky relayed Dan's answer, "I'm not dead."

"You are dead. Look down at your hands. Yeah exactly. What the f*#!, they are Deanna's hands," Ricky said.

"Why won't they talk to me?" Ricky said Danny asked.

"He was agitated and angry that no one would talk to him because he didn't realize he had died," Ricky said. A knowing awareness came over Deanna as she realized that he'd been frustrated because nobody would talk to him after he'd died. However, she did, even talking out loud to him. His signs became more persistent as his anger at being ignored grew. He hadn't known that he had died.

After a moment Ricky began speaking to each person in the room as if he was Danny. Looking at one of his sisters he said, "I will get you that teddy bear." Unbeknownst to Deanna, teddy bear was the nickname she had called her ex-boyfriend who Danny hadn't liked. To his brother, he said, "I'm shocked you are here, thanks for coming. I was in the bar dude. I kept trying to talk to you. I'd yell, but you didn't know I was there." His brother is a bartender. To Deanna's best friend, Bern, he said, "Thank you, just thank you." She was Deanna's rock through everything. Finally, looking at Deanna he said, "You are the only one who has always been there for me. I knew I could count on you. Tell Carmen, I'm sorry. He is a good guy."

Following a brief pause, Ricky said, "Deanna do you want him to leave?"

"Yes, I need you to leave," Deanna said. Afterwards, Deanna began feeling extremely anxious and nervous. Her body began to tingle and she was drawn down into a fetal position. Legs drawn up and unable to pick her shoulders up, Deanna asked, "What is wrong with me?" feeling as though she had no control of her body. She reached out and grabbed Danny's brother's hand.

"Who is the older lady, a family member with arthritis, smoking a cigarette?" Ricky asked. Danny's brother said, "That is our memom." Deanna's hands began trembling and she was overcome with fear.

"Are you scared Dan?" Ricky asked.

"Yes, he is scared, I can feel it," Deanna answered as her body began shaking more violently. She realized that his memom was there to help him cross over and that is why earlier she kept asking about memom.

"He's scared that she's mad at him because of the drugs and everything," Ricky said. Everyone in the room watched in amazement as Deanna appeared to be going through massive drug withdrawal at warp speed, her body convulsing uncontrollably. Suddenly, she began heaving and the room reeked of vomit, although physically she had not thrown up. After a few minutes, her body began to relax and she was overcome with exhaustion. Everyone in the room was stunned.

For days, Deanna felt empty. Although she thought that Dan had crossed over, she was a little worried that she hadn't done something right and inadvertently held him back. Therefore, she made an appointment to follow up with Ricky in his office. After hearing from Danny and being assured that he had crossed, Deanna voiced her concern about her daughter's inability to deal with his death. Ricky invited Gianna in and asked her if she wanted to talk to Danny. She did.

"I'm seeing Gianna as a little girl, like two or three. He's showing me tattoos. Did she ask about them?" Ricky asked.

"Yeah, that was the time he was really in her life and she did point and ask about them," Deanna said.

"He's saying Danny Boy," Ricky said. Gianna smiled at hearing the nickname she had given him. "He's saying that he was with you at his grave and he's showing me that you, Gianna, put a really big, bright flower there."

Both smiled and Deanna said, "Yeah, she gave him a sunflower."

"He's saying that he feels much better, that he is ok. Deanna felt relief encompass her knowing that Danny had now realized that he had died and saw them visiting his grave.

"He's showing me a stuffed animal with big floppy ears, maybe a bunny," Ricky said. "No there's no bunny," Deanna said, confused.

Gianna spoke up and said, "Mom, my Build-a-Bear." After he had died, Deanna had taken her to Build-A-Bear. Gianna had made a dog that had big floppy ears, which she had named Danny.

"Well, he saw it. Did you make him a card?" Ricky asked Gianna.

"Yeah, I did," Gianna said.

"You did?" Deanna asked unaware that she had.

"Yeah, with smiley faces and I told him that I missed him and that I'd cherish our memories together," Gianna said with a smile.

"Well he got it," Ricky said soothingly.

"He's saying that he wants you to do well in school and be good. School is very important and he's showing me a frog with speckles on it," Ricky added.

"There's nothing with a frog that I can remember," Deanna said perplexed.

Ricky finished by saying to Gianna, "He's showing me holding you up in the air, on a pedestal, that he'll always protect you. He's saying thank you, you taught him how to be a dad." Both mother and daughter cried for losing a man they had both loved, for being able to say goodbye, and finally for knowing that he was no longer in pain.

After returning home, Gianna showed her mom the card she had made and kept in her room. Later in the week, Deanna was going through a box of letters and cards. She pulled out a back-to-school-night letter from Gianna's first grade year. Deanna had written we are so proud of you and Danny had written "keep up the good work in school, love Danny Boy." On the letter was a frog that Danny and Gianna had colored in with speckles.

Deanna and her home are now at peace. There are no more phone calls, emails, moved pictures, or any other unexplainable events. She and Carmen are as happy as they'd been when they first married. Although the unsettling and hard to believe events were stressful, Deanna feels that maybe it all happened for a reason. Unable to let go of each other in the past, she feels that if she hadn't been there when Dan crossed over, she may have never accepted it.

Happy that he is free from his addiction and at peace, Deanna has let him go. She no longer fears death or questions that our spirits live on.

Here is what Deanna has to say about her experiences with Ricky:

"My experience with Ricky was amazing. Prior to meeting with him my emotions were a mess. He calmed both me and my daughter as he quickly helped us get through our loss. Knowing that our loved one is at peace, we started to smile again. We're forever grateful to have had this opportunity to receive Ricky's gift of helping and healing."

Deanna Dicampli

Danny & Deanna

Gianna horsing around with her Danny Boy

Daniel C. Stahl "Danny Boy"

Q & A with Ricky

What do you personally call spirits who have not crossed over after physical death?

"I call them 'ethereally challenged spirits.'"

Really what do you call them?

"Yes, there are 'earthbound' spirits."

Ok. In this story, Danny was "earthbound" and un-aware that his physical body had died from tainted drugs. From your experience, do a lot of earth-bound spirits remain because they did not know or expect death because it was very abrupt?

"It has been my experience that whether it is drugs, suicide, or a car accident, it all depends on their belief system and how aware they are of the 'afterlife.' If grandmom, best friend, or mom and dad are in the light, they will try their best to get them to come into the light. People who have the belief and that type of background tend to not be earthbound spirits because they have more of an association to the light. Now the ones who have a lot of guilt, shame, want revenge, or just plain don't want to leave that life will be more apt to be earthbound."

Does it sometimes happen that the person who ex-perienced physical death knows that they died but they did not want to "leave" a loved one who was still physically alive?

"I'll tell you this, there's not much difference

between being alive and being dead to a lot of these spirits. This is my perception, not my experience since I've not been dead, at least in this lifetime. Let's say that you love ice-cream, and you eat ice-cream morning, noon, and night and all of a sudden a rock fell out of the sky and killed you instantly. I mean, that fast. You'd be like, whoa. You don't really have a body but you are still looking for that ice-cream. You know death is kind of a state of mind."

So then, it really doesn't seem like a big deal for a spirit if they really are attached to a person here and don't want to leave them. For the spirit, is it still kind of like still being alive?

"Yeah, to some degree."

From your experience with earthbound spirits, do they seem to "attach" themselves to a physically "alive" human? If so, is this because they want to be in light? Why can't they just roam around?

"Ok. Let's put it this way. I believe there is a place that spirits go and we can call it heaven, the light, another dimension, or whatever you like. But, if you are highly or heavily addicted or that type of thing, your mind set is not about peace and love. It is about getting the next 'fix,' so they attach themselves to what I'll say is a human host. They kind of 'slime' them. In other words, you can't go and have a hamburger if you are a spirit. Someone may say that there are spirit hamburgers in heaven, but if you are earthbound you aren't in heaven. So you attach to someone so that you can have that hamburger, taste that hamburger, and experience those things. Also, if you don't really believe in heaven or you don't believe in the light and you are confused, you may go to the quickest source of light. That could be a loved one or someone like that because at least there is light there. Or let's say that a guy passes and his wife is the most important thing to him and she has always been dependent upon him, and she is weeping and doesn't know what to do. There might be a possibility of attachment there. Notice I said possibility, it doesn't always happen."

The concept of a spirit "attaching" to you can be a scary notion for a lot of people, although not as much if it is a loved one. Even unintentionally, can we inadvertently be welcoming this because we are missing them so much and wishing for them to be with us?

"Yes."

Ok. Do you have any advice for people on how to mourn without welcoming our loved ones to remain earthbound?

"Well, have them embrace the fact that they are going to a better place and that there are relatives there that have passed on who are loving and kind."

So actually talk to them and say to them you've died..."

"You can say, *'I'll see you soon, I love you.' 'I'll miss you, but I'll be ok,'* or whatever you need to say."

You've stated before that you don't know how spirits manipulate the physical world, but Danny was extremely active in doing so. From your experiences, is this unusual?

"Yes, it doesn't happen with everything and everybody, but it does happen, maybe not as extreme. It has been my experience as of late that a lot of spirits will hang out for a small amount of time and they will check in on you and make sure you are ok."

Is this the time between physical death and the crossing into the light?

"Yes, this usually happens right after a physical death."

When you were facilitating Danny's crossing over, you told him that he had died, and then Deanna asked him to leave. After this, she displayed physical signs of withdrawal (shaking, the smell of vomit, etc) as he was departing. Why?

"Actually this was happening almost simultaneously. He was pretty much affecting her entire energy field. He was attached to her so you could smell vomit, you know a drug addict vomiting, the shaking, and the withdrawal. And you can think of it this way. If you are hanging around with someone smoking a whole lot of cigarettes, you are going to smell like smoke."

Ok, that makes sense. In your opinion, is the phenomenon of "earthbound spirits" much more common than we think?
"I don't know. How would I know?"

Ok. Well then, out of all of the readings you've done what is the percentage?
"Seven. (Laughter) I would say to you from my experience, it is about five to ten percent."

Is it possible for earthbound spirits to cross over at any time, regardless of how long they have been earthbound?
"Uh-huh."

So they could be earthbound for four hundred years and then cross over?
"Yes."

Is the eventual crossing over because it was facilitated, like you did, or how else could they 'wake up?' What would make someone realize they're really dead after four hundred years?
"You seem actually angry about that question."

No.
"Are you confused?"

Yes.

"Ok, well you are probably as confused as many people. It has been my experience and what I have learned is that they can attach pretty much to a soul for several lifetimes."

Oh, so even when a person physically dies, a spirit can still be 'attached' to their spirit?

"To the essence of that spirit. Let's say in other words that you were Bob, the carpenter, and you died. And in your next life you were Sally, the homemaker. Well that spirit will still keep seeking you out."

So that spirit doesn't get born into a physical body, it can just keep following you around?

"Uh-huh."

Ok, well how can you discourage spirits from attaching to yourself?

"There are a couple of things. There are some great books out there that can be read and I would say to keep your own field as clear as you can. One of the ways to not have the spirit attach is to have a healthy lifestyle to the best of your ability. I think it can be a big deal for teenagers because they have a tendency to drink and do drugs to the point of passing out, and when you do that, you are opening yourself up for any funky thing out there to attach itself to you."

If someone is having a similar experience like this story, what advice would you give them? Would you tell them to speak to the spirit themselves, or get professional help from someone who can facilitate spirit release?

"I would say that if it is a spirit of a loved one, that they probably want to be heard in some way, shape, or form. You could seek someone out with a background in spirit release, or something like that. You can always acknowledge that they are there. Say to them that this is not the place for you now, and I will greet you in the light. Just to let them know to seek out the light. You know if Grandma was your favorite person in the world, seek her out. But remember that our own crazy lifestyles attract some of these spirits that had crazy lifestyles to begin with. So remember that spirit attachment isn't always because your best friend died. I remember years ago, a friend of mine showed me a picture of her standing in a bar after the bar closed and you could see light trails and spots of light everywhere. Bars and clubs are filled with that kind of stuff because sometimes spirits still want to party."

So basically if a loved one passes, you say to talk to them and encourage them to go towards the light and move on. For the ones you might not know to help avoid attachment, lead a healthy lifestyle. Is there any other advice?

"The other thing too, maybe not for sudden death, but if someone has cancer or a sickness, help prep them. This society does nothing about prepping people for the light and if we do, it is done through guilt. So depending on someone's religion, they may be taught you must repent and all of that stuff. This can have people get caught up in all the misery in their life, and that causes an area of guilt. If you are caught up in an area of guilt, you aren't in an area of love. You want to encourage them and let them know that there will be loved ones who will greet them."

12

Better Than A Million Dollars

Some of us take for granted that we are loved by our parents. It is easy when they are loving, attentive, and involved in our daily lives growing up. For all of you that had a less than perfect childhood, you are constantly aware of the scars that this can inflict on your soul for the rest of your life. Always remember that there is someone else out there who survived far worse atrocities during their childhood, yet they manage to grow into an incredibly beautiful adult. I found one such person who humbles me with her kind and loving spirit. I am honored to know Barbara Hawkins and share with you her story of how she met Ricky.

A friend at work had ranted and raved about this amazing psychic she'd met named Ricky Wood. Barbara had been to a psychic once about twenty years prior, and although she believed that some people had the ability, she found it hard to believe that this one was so special. Her friend had recently lost her father, and she told Barbara how he had come through in her reading. The details that Ricky gave had blown her away, and she'd known that it really was her father speaking to her. Barbara listened and found it interesting, but she didn't feel a need to see Ricky especially since she didn't understand how a medium worked.

A short while later, Barbara was having some family issues involving her children so she decided to give Ricky a call to see if he could shed any light on the situation. While calling to make the appointment, she was stunned when Ricky specifically referenced her reason for wanting to see him. Barbara became excited knowing that he was obviously the real deal. Solely focusing on helping her children, she did not expect to get any messages about her own childhood.

When Barbara arrived for her appointment, Ricky's kind and calming presence put her at ease immediately. Ready to talk about her children, she was shocked when the first thing Ricky said to her was, "I see royalty. Who is from royalty?" She couldn't believe it! Her mother was from a royal family in France. Barbara's great, great grandparents were a royal family that was extremely wealthy. This floored Barbara since she knew little of her blood line having grown up in foster care and orphanages.

When she was just two years old, Barbara became a ward of the state. Her father had been shot in the service, and he was in a VA hospital for an extended period of time with a severed leg. During this time her mother, an alcoholic, abandoned Barbara along with her two brothers who were four years and six months old. Even after being released from the hospital, her father did not return for her because he was told that his children were better off with families that could take care of them.

Ricky began speaking again and Barbara looked up at him. "Marion. Who is Marion?" he asked.

"That is my mom," she said amazed. "It really is her. Wow! I can't believe it," Barbara thought, her heart beginning to race.

"Your mom is saying that she is sorry she couldn't be the mother that you deserved. She's sorry that she couldn't give you the love that you deserved," Ricky said, his voice full of emotion. Barbara did not respond to Ricky. She couldn't believe what he was saying or how hearing from her mother was possible.

Hearing Ricky talking about her mother, Barbara immediately felt as if she was being transported back to when she was a little girl. Even after all of this time, she distinctly remembered the day her mother had left. Memories of going to the courthouse to wait for a visit with her mom flashed through her mind, but she never came. Barbara remembered the one gift her mom had mailed to her when she was eight. A little pink crocheted pocket book that she cherished so much she left it wrapped in the tissue paper. It had given her hope that her mom did love her and that she would come back and save her from the hell she was in. Barbara kept it in a drawer until one day when her foster mother threw it away.

At the time, Barbara was in one of the most abusive foster care families she'd encountered. She was forced to wear the same set of clothes for a month until they were ant ridden. When this happened, her foster mother would scratch her face and say, "I'm gonna make you ugly. You're gonna be a no-good-whore just like your mother." Barbara vividly remembered the embarrassment and shame she felt when she would wet the bed. Her foster care mother would make her stand naked in the front door while reprimanding her. Afterwards, she made Barbara place the soiled underpants in her mouth while walking to school until the crossing guard removed them. Shivering, Barbara pushed the awful memories of all of the injustices she had survived from her mind. These were but a few of the many.

By the age of twelve, the state had taken Barbara from the mentally ill woman's home and placed her in an orphanage. It had been like heaven compared to the foster homes she had endured. The only thing that had gotten Barbara through them was telling herself that if only her mom knew, she would come back and save her. No matter what anyone said, she knew that her mom loved her and that she would come back one day.

Barbara had never given up hope. Every year

when the new phone book would come, she would call every one with her last name, which was Love. She was always met with, "No, I'm not your mother," or "You called me last year. No, I am still not your Mother. Stop calling," she heard over and over. She began to give up hope. However, when she was eighteen and did her annual calling, a man answered and asked, "Is this Barbara?" When she replied, "Yes," she heard, "I'm your father." She eagerly went to visit him, only to encounter his girlfriend and new children who were far less than happy to meet her. Shortly after, her father asked her to stop coming around. During their brief reunion, Barbara did learn that he knew where her mother was. He told her she could find her in Margate, New Jersey.

Barbara was brought back to the present when Ricky continued speaking. "She is asking for your forgiveness. She needs your forgiveness to move on," Ricky said. Barbara was shocked. She'd never thought of forgiving her. It had taken years of trying to forgive and let go of all of the awful things the numerous foster families had put her through. But she'd never thought that her mom would want forgiveness especially since Barbara had found her again before her death.

When she was eighteen, she and her girlfriend took the information her father had given her and took a bus to Margate, New Jersey. After searching numerous bars, she found her in one named Maynard's. There was her mother, in all her glory, standing on top of the bar singing "Hello Dolly." For the next two years Barbara went to see her many times hoping that they could connect, but to her dismay she only saw her mother sober for about half an hour the entire time. Marion had no interest in being the mommy that Barbara always longed for. Each visit was the same with her intoxicated mother accompanied by the mayor, owner of the boat yard, or some other wealthy man. Finally, when Marion went as far as to fix Barbara's husband up with other women, Barbara had enough. Realizing that she would never have the mom she'd waited for her whole life, Barbara gave up.

Suddenly, she realized that Ricky had begun speaking again. "She wants you to know that she loves you. And although she didn't show it, she always loved you," Ricky said looking into Barbara's eyes. Those words echoed in her head as she thought, "She did?" Barbara had never known. Her heart ached for all the years that she had wanted to hear this. Slowly, it felt as if the ache was being replaced with a warmness that filled up her heart. Barbara had waited half her life to hear those words from her mother and they seemed to touch the center of her soul. It was as if in an instant, her hope had been restored. All of those years that she felt deep down that her mom loved her, she was not wrong. Alcoholism had been the reason she could not show it. As tears spilled from her eyes, Barbara felt that hearing those words was better than being handed a million dollars.

Although feeling years away, she refocused on Ricky because he was speaking again. "There are siblings but you don't know each other. How are there siblings and you don't know each other?" Ricky asked.

For the first time during the reading, Barbara responded to Ricky. "We were separated when we went into foster care homes," she replied.

"So this all has made sense so far?" Ricky asked not knowing if anything he had said made any sense to her.

"Oh yes, very much so," Barbara said in awe that Ricky knew things that most people didn't. She thought of her youngest brother Bobby and the day of her mother's funeral.

After two years of unsuccessfully trying to reconnect with her mom, Barbara stopped going to see her. A couple of years later, she received a call that her mother was dying from cirrhosis of the liver. The day of the funeral, Barbara found only herself and Bobby standing next to her coffin. In a detached manner they compared their mother's physical traits to their own. Bobby, who was only six months old when his mother left, had been with one foster care family that raised him well. Of all the siblings, he had the most normal childhood; however, they never told him that he had any siblings other than the sister he had from them. Looking at her mother's body, Barbara thought, "Life just sucks." Along with her mother, Barbara's hopes of having her mom love her like she wanted her to died. Although

Barbara and her brothers had found each other, a distance remained between them.

Ricky wasn't finished with his message to her. He said, "Barbara, you have a good life now and a good husband. Stop worrying so much over your kids. It's time to worry about yourself. Enjoy life." Barbara smiled and thought of her life now. She had a wonderful and loving husband. She knew Ricky was right but she found it hard to not fret over her children's happiness, although they were adults. After the hellish childhood she'd endured, her children were her world. She never wanted them to feel the pain that she had.

For a week following her session with Ricky, Barbara thought about everything he had told her. She forgave her mother. Although she hadn't even realized that she needed to do it, Barbara found it to be a very healing experience. Finally she was able to face the little girl inside after all those years. The tears of pain and abandonment were replaced with the loving words from her mother.

Since that day, Barbara's outlook on life has changed. Having let go of the pain she felt around her mother and family, Barbara is trying to reconnect and get to know her brothers better. No longer trying to forget, she now is able to allow herself to think of her mother and father, not as a little girl but as an adult. Barbara no longer fears death as she has realized that it is merely a transition of her spirit. Barbara is truly grateful for Ricky and the gifts that he has given her.

Here is what Barbara has to say about her experiences with Ricky:

"Ricky was so warm and comfortable to talk to. He was right to the point and very honest. My session with Ricky was better than a million dollars as he had no idea of the rejection and pain I had always felt from my mother's abandonment. To have her come through to ask for my forgiveness and say she loved me was indeed a shock, bringing so much healing. Thank you Ricky, I finally found my real mother and the love I knew she had for me after all these years."

Barbara Hawkins

Barbara's mother Marion is 2nd from the left.

Marion DeSaussure Lynah Love

Q & A with Ricky

When you were giving Barbara this information in her session, did you know all of this about her childhood or how what you were saying was connected?

"No, it was the first time I'd ever met her and she didn't tell me the information you have in your story."

In general, do you remember what you say in your readings?

"Sometimes a little, but it would be like trying to remember every name of every person you ever met. You couldn't. So no, not really."

Does seeing the connection now with Barbara's life, and how what you said changed it for the better surprise you?

"No."

Ok, does it humble you?

"You know, if I can help anybody it is very humbling because it amazes me. I mean, I don't sit around going *I know what to do, I know what to do*...I am just giving them the information. So if I help anyone it is a gift."

Well it is kind of amazing the information you give without even realizing the connection. It is really neat. Unfortunately many children are scarred during childhood from absent, addicted, or abu-

sive parents. For some, it seems to break them and they follow in their parents destructive footsteps. Yet for others they become the complete opposite and are incredible, loving, and attentive parents. Do you have an opinion as to why this happens and what the difference is?

"I think that is up to the individual. Also I want to say that we all have people who come into our lives. They seem to come at the right place and the right time to help us out. It might have been a school teacher for you; it might have been a friend for me. In other words, the laws of attraction pretty much dictate that you can attract to you what you need. Another way to look at it is, let's say we are all hanging out in heaven and we decide to go back. So we have people who love us there who come back too and seek us out to try and help us. They come in different ways at different times. It depends on whether we are ready to receive that. We all have angels. Everybody thinks that angels are beings with wings that exist on another plane. But sometimes we all as human beings have the ability to be angels. You know you start a foundation to help kids who are hungry, or you start a mentorship program. That's why we are on this planet, to find ways to help improve life."

So you think there are many factors? I mean I am just amazed at what Barbara had to endure as a child and what an incredible person and parent she turned out to be. A lot of people that have to endure that type of childhood turn out to be very angry, drug addicted, or what have you.

"But, I guarantee you with Barbara that there are beings of light on this plane and that plane that came in to help her."

In your experience, when they come through, do parents who have not been very good parents realize this and regret their actions? Or are they like "Oh well, I did they best I could".

"I heard something a long time ago from a man who said *that all of us wound our kids in one way or another.* If we were perfect then the kids would be perfect and we don't want perfection, we want knowledge and wisdom. Having knowledge and wisdom is the biggest gift, and even if our parents weren't the best, the most loving, if we can get beyond that and move forward, in a way it could be a gift.

Now, when I read people that have been abused and their parents come through, I think they are very apologetic. Once you go to a place of love, heaven, or whatever you want to call it, you are surrounded by love. So imagine being extremely angry in a place of love, it doesn't really work. But the parts of your personality that were angry and cranky may come through because if not, no one would be able to understand anything if they didn't give a name or an identifier to who they were.

Most of them realize that they did do the best with what they had. Like the old adage, *'if you can walk a mile in my shoes then you can judge me.'* We have no idea what was going on with the parents. It doesn't mean it is an excuse at all; it is just that some are saying this is what happens. And here's something else. Would that person have started a foundation if their life was completely happy all the time and there was no abuse around them?"

Probably not.

While you were talking something seemed to click for me when you said, 'When spirits are in a place of love it is hard to be angry.' From my experience, the reason that people are angry, or sad, or addicted all comes from fear.
    "Yes."

So when you are in the light or heaven, you realize that there is nothing to fear like you do as a physical human being. Is that why it is easier to see the big picture? You no longer fear death or anything so fear dissipates, and therefore the anger and the sadness go. Is that kind of how it works?
    "That could be a great way to look at it."

You've said previously that a lot of the information you get is a feeling, not always words, or pictures (although in this story you did give Marion's name). A repeating theme throughout most of the stories is that the spirits coming through want to let the person in session with you know just how much they love them. Could you try to put into words how that comes across to you? Do you feel overwhelming love? How do you know that?

"People communicate in different ways. Personalities are different. Some people are very verbal. Some are very emoting. Some people do it with pictures. Some do it with symbols. If dad wasn't the hugging-squeezing-feely type, but if he shows you a picture of the first puppy he ever bought you, you will feel that feeling."

That must be a very rewarding part of your job to see and feel that love that you are conveying. Is that one of the reasons you do it?

"Yes. It is the best feeling in the world. It also lets you know that you're not crazy. So when every skeptic or every person steps up and says that's crazy, that's impossible, you're using these people, you're hurting those people, there is something about the feeling that you get, and that the people get that changes everything. It lets you know that what you are doing is right."

13

An Angel Like No Other

For most of us, when we lose a loved one unfairly and abruptly, we are unable to move forward. Instantly the pain and numbness feels as though our mind, body, and souls are encompassed in concrete. Even if prior to the loss you felt an understanding and openness to the continued existence of our spirits, tragedy can thwart this. Allowing someone else into your heart can help.

Anne Belle had met Ricky at a party and she was amazed by his abilities. Her friend, Mathy, was despondent and in an indescribable amount of pain. Anne told her that she thought a session with Ricky might help her. Although Mathy believed that there were psychic mediums that had authentic abilities, she had never felt the need to go see one. She came from a spiritual family that embraced their own abilities to receive messages from those who have crossed over.

After four months, Mathy didn't seem to be

getting any better, so Anne continued to try and persuade her to have a session with Ricky. Mathy felt she was at a point that she could let someone else in, so she agreed and asked Anne to make her an appointment. Anne called and told Ricky that she was bringing a friend in. She did not give him any other information, as Mathy had requested.

As they were driving to Ricky's office, Anne's phone rang. Ricky said, "Tell your friend not to feel so tense. She'll be fine. It'll be fine." After Anne hung up the phone and told Mathy what he said, she was amazed. Anne had not given Ricky any information except that she was bringing someone to see him. He had not been told whether the friend was male or female, whether she was married, had children, or what purpose she had for coming to see him.

Calmness enveloped Mathy's body as she was reminded of the dreams she had about Ricky. After the second one, she knew that she was supposed to meet him. In her dreams she clearly saw his unique physical features. When they arrived at his office, she saw him standing in the parking lot and she immediately went up to him and said, "Hi Ricky, I'm Mathy." He looked almost identical to the images that she had seen in her dreams. He was about 5'7 with bronze colored skin and black curly hair. His eyes were welcoming and his presence calming. She knew that this was where she was supposed to be.

Mathy sat down across from Ricky once inside

his office. "You should be doing what I'm doing," Ricky said as he recognized her spirituality and ability to tap into other planes (a side that goes undeveloped by most people). Mathy felt instantly at ease, sensing that there was no where else she should be at this moment.

"I see a little girl and she is just playing, playing, playing." Ricky smiled as he said, "She's happy and she loves to play ball! She is just as happy as she can be and she is playing with other kids," Ricky continued seeming to enjoy the picture. "She really loves ball. She plays a lot of ball," he said trying to stress the abundance of joy he felt around this child.

Mathy smiled knowing that Anne was right and Ricky was authentic. She thought about her daughter Candace as she did every day. She was such a happy girl who played on the soccer, basketball, and the lacrosse team. Candace would say, "Lets go catch ball," to her dad whom she played softball with all the time. She also played tennis and swam in the summers. Ricky began speaking again.

"But there is something wrong, there is a problem with her heart," Ricky said as a concerned look clouded his face.

"Yeah, she had a heart defect, an organic murmur. This child had pulmonary stenosis," Mathy responded as she recalled the diagnosis Candace had been given at eight months old. It was an obstruction in the heart that caused her heart rate to go very high when she was sick or in a lot of pain.

Suddenly Ricky gasped. "What is this? I don't understand," he said as he began to appear visibly agitated. "Why do I see suicide and depression? This child is not depressed! She is a very, very happy child. This doesn't make sense!" Ricky said emphatically appearing angry as he couldn't discern how she was there one minute and gone the next. As Mathy drew in a breath, it felt as if her heart had momentarily stopped. For a split second she felt as if Ricky was seeing through her eyes. He was feeling the emotional pain laced with confusion and anger that had encased her for the last four months.

"You're right," Mathy responded sadly. "She was not depressed, she was put on anti-depressants not for depression, but for anxiety, and she did take her own life." Mathy already knew unequivocally that Candace was not depressed and that the drugs she was prescribed caused it. At that moment she felt understood watching Ricky's reaction. After a roller coaster ride of medications, Candace met an untimely death.

He felt the anger and utter disbelief that she had been feeling since that horrific day. Mathy gasped as she saw Ricky connect with the feeling of someone reaching in and ripping out a piece of her heart that could never be replaced. She placed her hand over her heart as if to protect the raw scar that will forever remain.

Unable to put into words the depth of her pain and sorrow, Mathy felt validated. If she had lost

Candace to her heart condition, she knows she would feel the same void; however, the abruptness and lack of awareness that something like this could happen added to the complete devastation that penetrated to the depths of her soul.

"Candace is so loving, compassionate, and helpful to others," Ricky stated seeming to be taken away from the ending of her physical life onto describing her soul and legacy. He continued, "She always put others before herself. She was a welcomer and a teacher." Mathy felt as if she was in the midst of a huge déjà vu moment. Candace's teacher had used the identical words to describe her at her service. Hearing it again, Mathy was struck by the beautiful and mature attributes that were used to describe her twelve year old. Her heart swelled with love for her daughter.

"Mathy," Ricky continued, "I see you standing at a podium in front of hundreds of people. BE STRONG. You have to be strong because they want to see your tears." Ricky continued adamantly, "You have got to be strong. You can't cry in front of them because that is what they want to see."

After being given additional messages from Candace, Mathy stood and embraced Ricky. A wave of knowing washed over her as she felt that she had met him for a reason. She knew that there was a spiritual connection and she wondered why she had fought coming to see him. The words "the right time, the right place" popped into her head.

Six months later, Mathy was standing at a podium in front of hundreds of people addressing the FDA. She stood tall and strong telling them, "I am not impressed with you sitting back in your ivory towers passing judgment on our children, and our children's blood is on your hands." She did not cry. This statement was replayed in the New York Times, World News Tonight, Fox, MSNBC, and the Today Show. Even at a medical conference, the head speaker quoted her in discussing the corruption of the drug industry in marketing drugs, over medication in our society, and how they are being used to make a buck.

A black box warning appeared on the drug within two weeks of a video of Candace being aired on TV. It was undeniable that this was not a girl who struggled with depression. Candace was a happy, friendly, and vibrant girl. A week after Mathy's address, she recalled Ricky's statement to her during their session. She was floored because she hadn't given it any thought since that day. She was amazed that he had been able to see how events were going to unfold in her future.

Candace continues to make her presence known to all those she loves. She has given so many of them signs that are indisputable. One such event occurred in front of nineteen witnesses. Candace's family and friends went to the beach to celebrate her birthday. During the drive, her friends joked about what signs they might get from her, as they had all experienced ones from her previously.

As they gathered in a circle and sang Happy

Birthday to her, they threw flowers in the ocean and let go of the twenty-two balloons they had purchased for her. In awe, they watched as the balloons slowly rose into the sky above the ocean and formed a huge C. They looked at each other to see if each was seeing the same thing. They all did. Again, skeptically thinking that maybe it was a coincidence, they contemplated the possibility that the wind current caused them to form into the first letter of Candace's name. Shortly after, the same balloons had dispersed and resembled into an unmistakable number 9. Candace's nine best friends were in attendance. What a great gift each received that day.

Ricky has helped give Mathy the confidence to embrace her power to move forward. Candace and her legacy will live on forever. The abrupt loss of such a beautiful young girl is a terrible tragedy, but her death will not be in vain. The strength and determination that her family has shown will save countless lives. Although her physical presence is greatly missed by so many, Candace's loving spirit is very much alive.

Here is what Mathy has to say about her experiences with Ricky:

"My beautiful little girl had only been gone a few months. My pain remained so intense that I sometimes felt that I could not live through the day, that the pain would kill me. If it had not been for my surviving daughter, I think it might have. A dear friend kept mentioning Ricky and told me that seeing him would make me feel better and diminish my agony. I did not believe her. Nothing could help. She finally convinced me to go with her. It was almost a three hour drive and a couple of states away. I think she thought it would do me good just to get out of the house. Nothing could have prepared me for what happened next.

I had had several dreams about Ricky, this person I did not know, and yet I knew him the minute I saw him. It was the person from my dreams. We met up with Ricky outside of the building, yet I walked right up to him and introduced myself. I wore no jewelry, including my wedding band, and had on a track suit, something I would not ordinarily wear. I wanted to give no clues as to who I was or my marital status. The minute that I sat down, this man started talking about my little girl. "I see a little girl and she's so happy! She's just playing, playing, playing. She loves to play ball." Wow! Candace played on the soccer team, basketball team, and the lacrosse team. When she wasn't playing sports, she could be found outside playing catch with her daddy. Then Ricky went on to talk about her little heart, how there was a problem. Yes, she had pulmonary stenosis, an obstruction in her heart that not everyone knew about. The final shock came when he suddenly said, "Wait a minute! What is this? Why do I see suicide and depression? This is a happy child! What is going on?" These last statements took my breath away! How could Ricky possibly have known that my beautiful, happy little girl had hanged herself at the age of 12 years old, with no history of depression or suicidality? Candace had been prescribed an antidepressant for test anxiety at school. We had never been warned that antidepressants kill up to 4 out of every 100 children. Now there is a Black Box Warning on all antidepressants, but at the time, no warnings were ever given. The last major statement that I remember from that first visit was Ricky telling me that he saw me standing at a podium, addressing hundreds of people. Ricky kept telling me, "Be strong! Do not shed tears in front of them. They want to see you weak. BE STRONG!" I thought Ricky was crazy. I teach second grade. I am used to speaking to children and had never addressed an audience for anything in my life. But true to Ricky's word, six months later, almost to the day, I stood before the FDA at the hearings on adverse reactions that children experience on antidepressants; risks that we learned had first been noted at the FDA hearings in 1991, the year Candace was born. As my husband and I stood before the FDA panel, with hundreds of people behind us, I told them "The blood of our children is on your hands." That comment was picked up by the New York Times and repeated in the news all over the United States. I have continued to speak out. Thanks, Ricky, for giving me the strength and understanding to move forward. Together we are making a difference!"

Mathy Downing

Candace with her family -
Mom- Mathy, Sister -Caroline, and Dad-Andy

Candace at one of her favorite places-- the beach.

Candace Leigh Downing

Q & A with Ricky

In this story, it seems that your friend, Candace, breaks a lot of the molds. For example, in Chapter Two we discussed suicide in its better known form -- the result of depression. Yet, here is a little girl with no history of depression. It sounds as if Candace was a victim of big business and pharmaceutical drugs, not depression, hopelessness, and self-inflicted physical death. Do you agree?

"I would say that Candace is one of the happiest spirits I've ever met. She does not hold any of the despondency that I've experienced with spirits who have committed suicide. So to answer your question, yes, I do think there was a medical mistake made with this girl."

Candace has made it crystal clear that her spirit lives on with the many messages she gives to her family and friends. However, she seems happy, content, and in the "light" or place of love. She is not "earthbound"' as we discussed in Chapter Eleven, yet she has given countless physically manifested signs of her continued existence. You have said that you don't know how this is done, but how do you think this is possible?

"I believe it is the vibrancy of the child, and from what I understand, she was such a happy kid. Also, when I did the work with Candace, she was happy. Candace, without a doubt, is more of a teacher or guide spirit. You don't see it as much with children, but with her you do. There is a wisdom beyond her years. Also, there seems to be so many connections with Candace in my everyday life that I believe that she is a guardian angel to more than just me."

So Candace is a guardian angel to you?

"Yes, a teacher and a guide spirit. I think this child lovingly nudges me sometimes on a daily or weekly basis, depending on the time of the year."

Do you think she is able to physically manifest so much because she is so determined? Maybe because her death was so premature she is trying to give peace to her loved ones and let them know she is still "alive?"

"Yes, Candace has provided signs on many occasions, but I believe her being a guide and a teacher spirit is really more of her being around because she is assisting. She is helping guide people, make a statement, make a commitment, and to change the world. That is why she is around."

Could you clarify what a "teacher spirit" is?

"They are spirits that teach. (Chuckle) She is a teacher or guide spirit. She has a job to do, a mission. You could say that she transcended a lot faster. After she passed on, she is helping parents and other kids who have committed suicide. That has come out on more than one occasion. She has helped in many ways. I don't want to say 'fight the battle' because I don't really think she fights battles. She helps others, and defends people who can't defend themselves. Candace is one of the strongest spirits I've ever worked with. She has been support for her parents, she has been support for others, and she has appeared to others. I'm telling you, there is a reason why she was here, there was a reason why she left, and there is a reason why she is back, and all of it is good."

Losing a child has to be one of the most devastating events one can live through. What advice or words of comfort would you offer to parents who have experienced the loss of a child?

"Love them, honor them, cherish them, play with them, talk to them, and be with them as much as they can on this planet. If you lose a child, which is the most painful thing, know that there are loved ones on the other side to receive them, and there is nothing to worry about. Praying for them is a great thing, and it is not because you need to ask God to intercede, but because they will hear your prayers. Prayers are a very strong wavelength of communication."

Candace's family has taken their pain and used it as a force for good and change by tirelessly advocating for children and their parents' rights to the truth about the potential side effects of medications. Do you think if more people took this road, mankind would be in a better place overall?

"Yes. When I met with the family there was such a strong sense that Candace is not gone. This kid is so vibrant, and she is around family and other loved ones. There is a happiness and joy to her that just didn't leave. You know, 'love never dies,' and we hear that all the time but it truly doesn't and you can truly feel that energy and love coming from Candace. It is so strong. A kid's love is different. It is different than a spousal love. It radiates and you can feel, 'I love you Mommy. I love you Daddy.' That is why it is so important that we allow our kids to experience love -- less of our anger and more of our love."

So what do you think the difference is between the Downing family and others who are just as crushed by their loss? How they brought to fruition education and change, what do you think the difference is?

"I think the amazing thing is that with the Downing family, they were able to take their pain and suffering, lift it up, and then place it down. Maybe it was only for a minute at a time, maybe it was only for an hour at a time, but the more they realized how loving and how strong their daughter really was, there wasn't a sense of never seeing her again. That she was always ok, and she was always letting her parents know who she was and what she was doing. Candace in her own way was giving words of encouragement to her mother. I would get very specific messages from Candace to share with her family. I didn't understand what they meant and they would be almost over the top, you know, '*speaking in front of thousands,*' I had no idea. But Candace did…"

So you think it was their ability to take that pain and step forward with it?

"Yes. It was never an anchor. In other words they could feel it, but they didn't let it keep them from moving. It was sad, and the family went through extreme ups and downs, and there were times when it was crushing for them, but as time went on, they really did understand that there is life after death. They could feel it, and they could feel her. There is a very incredible loving presence with Candace. I've had my own run-ins with Candace. Candace has made herself known to me in ways I would never suspect and she continues to do so to this day."

Candace seems to be able to tirelessly reach so many with her messages and signs. Do you think this is because of her child-like spirit, that she doesn't see limitations or that she has a special calling to transform the world? In this story, we only gave a couple of examples of the very long list of messages that she has given, but why do you think she is able to do this more than other spirits seem to be able to do?

"I think we take for granted when one says, 'that's an old soul' but I believe that Candace has been around a lot more than others and lived many lifetimes. There is purity to her. I'm not going to say she is the messiah, but the energy of Christ is to help others and to express and show love. She carries a lot of that energy with her and she does it very eagerly. She is happy. Love is happy. And she wasn't tainted by anger. She had anxiety in her life, but she did not have a lot of anger. She has allowed herself to be utilized for the cause of peace and love and I think she is happy with that. I think any child would be happy with that. Most children are very, very caring. She is a great kid."

14
Veggie Tray

The simple times, like back-yard barbeques, watching football games, or just hanging out, can be some of our best memories. There is nothing like that feeling of joy when you share good food, good drinks, and plenty of laughter with the family. For Debbie Siple and her siblings, family gatherings like this were special when they were shared with their father, Robert Yeatman "a.k.a. Bob".

Bob, a patient and loving family man, was a softie when it came to his four daughters: Debbie, Barbara, Karen, and Judy, and his only son, Bobby Jr. Although he came from humble beginnings, Bob worked hard to give his children everything he could. He was kind and generous, easily giving into their wishes. Wanting to give them the best advantages in life, Bob and his wife paid for each of their children to attend college.

Unlike the typical role as the tough disciplinarian that many fathers take on, Bob was his children's friend. He left the stricter approach of child rearing to his wife Lucille. Described by his children as the "glue" that kept them together, Bob brought joy and love into their lives. When his grandchildren were born, he continued this by gladly embracing babysitting and helping out with anything he could.

Bob was a healthy and active man, so when he became ill and needed surgery to repair a ruptured bowel, his family was surprised. Being a nurse, Debbie was concerned, but not too worried because it wasn't a "risky" surgery, and he was otherwise very healthy. All went well with the surgery and after a couple weeks in the hospital, Bob went home to recover.

Debbie was startled when she received a call in the middle of the night from her mom saying that something was wrong with her dad. She lived only a couple of miles away so she was there for the CPR at the house, the ambulance ride, and the hour they worked on him at the hospital. Sitting at the head of his hospital bed when revival efforts were abandoned, Debbie had déjà vu recalling a dream she had about that very moment. One week after the successful surgery, Bob died from a pulmonary embolism.

The family was shocked and devastated. One month Bob was vibrant and healthy, and the next, he was gone. Debbie was beside herself because in her educated opinion as a nurse, she believed this would have been avoidable if he had been given

compression boots to wear after surgery to coun-
teract the development of blood clots.

In the few years following their dad's death,
each child felt a tremendous void. The family gatherings weren't the same without Bob's jovial and
hospitable manner. The joy that he brought to the
gatherings was gone, and although his children still
visited one another and remained close, their visits
were not as often, nor were they ever the same.

Although while growing up she was told that
it was "the work of the devil" and contradictory to
the teachings of the bible, Debbie always had an
interest in psychics and mediums. After her dad's
passing, she was even more drawn to them because of her yearning to hear from him again. She
did have a few psychic readings and believed in
the validity of such things, but Debbie had yet to
experience a reunion through a medium.

On her dad's September fifteenth birthday, just
four months following his passing, Debbie, her
mom, and siblings all went to a gallery event to see
psychic John Edwards in Philadelphia, Pennsylvania.
Each was excited to be sitting in the second row
anticipating hearing from Bob on his special day.
Although John read people all around them, he
did not get any information from Bob for his family.
They left intrigued by mediumship, but disappointed that they didn't get to hear from their dad.

Not too long after going to see John Edwards,
Debbie had a friend from work tell her about a
reading she had with a local psychic medium

named Ricky Wood. After hearing her rant and rave about the details he gave in her session, Debbie was interested, but didn't get in touch with him right away. When Ricky's name came up again some time down the road, she decided to give him a call. It took a while to coordinate everyone's schedule, but eventually they all agreed on a date and time to have him come to their mom and dad's house to do a group reading.

On a Saturday afternoon, all five of Bob's children, his wife Lucille, and daughter-in-law Denise, gathered at his house. Anxious to see if Ricky was the real deal, they nervously discussed what room to have the reunion in. Although it wasn't the place their family usually congregated, they all agreed on the formal living room because there weren't a lot of pictures there, and they didn't want to give Ricky any clues. They warned each other, especially Debbie, to remain tight-lipped and offer little to no information to Ricky.

When he arrived, Debbie answered the door since she had been the one who set up the reading. Ricky introduced himself and his warm and calm demeanor seemed to instantly ease some of her nerves. Debbie led him through the kitchen and into the formal living room.

"I really don't want to do it here," Ricky said appearing to be "feeling around" and sensing something they couldn't see. "I really sense a strong male presence here in the family room," Ricky said entering it. Debbie smiled. The family room held the TV where they gathered with dad to watch the football games, the tree at Christmas where they exchanged gifts, the fireplace, and many great memories.

Everyone was looking at Debbie with the "but-there-are-pictures-in-there" look so she said to Ricky, "Should I cover up the family picture?" referring to the large family portrait above the fireplace.

"No, but if you prefer I'll put my back to it," Ricky said assuring her.

While the others took their seats, Ricky began preparing for the reading by saying a prayer. Debbie went and retrieved the water bottles and vegetable tray she had hurriedly purchased earlier in the day. Caught up in the excitement, she hadn't thought of food or drinks until the last minute, so she just grabbed them from the grocery store on the way over.

Ricky began by asking, "Who are the skeptics?" The second oldest, Barb, raised her hand, followed by their mother Lucille. Both were seated the farthest away from where Ricky stood with his back to the fireplace. The two biggest believers, Debbie and her sister-in-law Denise, were on the couch right in front of him.

"I'm hearing an R word... Rehoboth. I used to live there so I'm sure that's it," Ricky said. No one said a word. Bob's wife, Lucille, didn't speak up although she spent many of her childhood summers there. She had come from an affluent family that was lucky enough to spend entire summers at the beach. Holding fast to their "not-giving-up-any-information" pact, everyone remained silent.

Ricky continued by talking about seeing military planes, the Korean War, and World War II. Again, there was no validation, so he kept going.

Ricky began seeing the stomach area, blood flowing, and choking during a procedure at the end of this spirit's physical life. His descriptions and gestures were pointing towards Bob's death, but it wasn't definitive enough, so no one in the room said anything while he continued. "He has a great sense of humor," Ricky said. "He wants to know what the heck is going on with this water and this veggie tray." Ricky said pointing towards it "He's saying that this is a pathetic party," Ricky added.

This made everyone laugh because they were not a health conscious bunch when it came to family gatherings. Tons of junk food, some alcoholic drinks, and a party type atmosphere were the norm for barbeques around Barb's pool, holiday and family gatherings. Debbie smiled at her out-of-the-ordinary choice of veggies and water.

"He's complaining about the lack of food and saying that this should be a barbeque," Ricky added. "There should be tons of food."

Ricky continued on, "I'm getting information on a boy...grandchild level...around the age of twenty-five and he has some type of respiratory problems. Is there anyone in the group that has a child with respiratory problem that is around the age of twenty-five?"

There's a pause and no one says anything. A few eyes begin to look at Deb. "Does it have to be his biological grandchild, or can it be a boyfriend or fiancé?" Debbie asked.

"Anyone that would be on the grandchild level, not just biological… This boy, he has health issues he is not taking care of what he needs to take care of. He is not as prepared as he should be in dealing with this illness. He needs to be more prepared and be more aggressive with his diet and supplementation." Ricky said matter-of-factly.

Everyone was still worried about not giving Ricky any hints so they remained silent. Although she didn't say a word, Debbie knew Ricky was referring to her daughter's fiancé, Josh, who is twenty-five and has cystic fibrosis.

"Come on guys, work with me here. If what I'm saying is ringing true, please let me know," Ricky said waiting for someone to validate if what he was saying was making sense.

"Now I'm hearing Betty Ann… or Barbara Ann?" Ricky said trying to decipher what he was hearing.

"That's me." Barb said raising her hand. Ricky had not been introduced to everyone when he arrived so the only name he knew in the room was Debbie's. Ricky started with her name but then quickly changed course. "He is saying, 'Can we party down a bit? Loosen up. This is supposed to be fun.'" Ricky pointed to Bobby. "He's saying you like to drink. You need to watch the drinking and just going to the doctor is not taking care of your-self." Laughing Ricky added, "Your dad is pissed about the veggie tray."

Everyone laughed and began to relax. It broke the ice, making them feel like their dad was joking with them. It was something he would have said if he were there. Beginning to feel a reconnection, all eyes were intent on Ricky as he continued.

"I'm getting an L name. Lynn....no..."

"My name is Lucille," Bob's wife said raising her hand.

"Ok, it is you then. He's saying he plays with you at the house by turning the lights off and on and the TV flickering."

"Oh my God....Ok," Lucille said knowingly as she became teary-eyed. She could no longer deny that she was hearing from her husband. It was her husband, Bob, talking to them through Ricky. She hadn't told anyone about the lights and TV-flickering-thing happening so her children were surprised to hear it.

"I see a dock and I see a man or a woman on a dock waving to the other one on a ship," Ricky said. Lucille could no longer fight her emotions and her tears spilled out as she felt transported back to when she had gone to Europe on the Queen Elizabeth while in college and Bob was at the dock waving to her when she left. Years later, when Bob went to the Korean War, Lucille was at the dock waving goodbye to him.

"He didn't believe in this stuff either," Ricky added. The air in the room began to transmute from one of skepticism to openness. The folded arms and non-belief began fading away. Everyone watched Ricky with intentness and curiosity wondering what their beloved dad would say next. "He wants to smack and hug all of you," Ricky said lightly, bringing chuckles and smiles from everyone.

Pausing for a moment, Ricky looked towards Barb and asked, "Are you married?"

"Yes," she responded.

"Someone from your spouse's family is coming through. I'm seeing a woman with spots on her hands. Veins and spots," Ricky said as he began to wring his hands. "She always did this," Ricky said continuing to wring his hands.

Barb's eyes widened in shock as she watched him. Her husband's grandmother had wrung her spot and vein covered hands identically to the way Ricky was doing it.

"That is my husband's grandmother," Barb offered.

"Let your husband know that his mom and dad are fine and they are still watching out for you guys," Ricky said. With that message seeming to be complete, Ricky paused and moved his gaze straight ahead.

Looking at Denise (Bobby's wife), "You are going to be OK. You just need to make decisions, and all of them will support you," Ricky said while motioning to the family. Looking to Bobby, Ricky said, "You need to be gentle with your wife." After a short pause Ricky continued.

"Your father's showing me sports... and the word... PING," Ricky said questioningly, unaware of what it meant. Bobby's face became flushed and his eyes filled with tears. His dad had been with him when he purchased his first set of golf clubs. The brand he bought was Ping. Ricky hadn't made the connection because he does not play golf.

"If I can make him cry, then I have done my job," Ricky said more as a message than a personal statement. He continued giving various messages from Bob to his family for a few more minutes.

Then Ricky said, "I have some woman pushing through now. I'm getting something with the brain," Ricky said moving his hands up to his head. "I'm sensing something wrong with the brain. Is there somebody with something wrong with their brain?" Ricky asked.

"Oh, could that be my son with epilepsy?" Debbie asked.

"Yeah," Ricky said after a pause, listening intently to someone they couldn't see. "The food is affecting him. Could be the dyes in his food... he needs natural foods, free from dyes, and additives. This could help him," Ricky said finishing that message.

"There is a dog with your dad, one that you grew up with." Ricky said. Everyone smiled thinking of their dog "Ronny." There is also another dog there that's a rude dog, the dog has passed, and something to do with humping," Ricky said kind of shrugging and chuckling. Debbie and her family all broke out in laughter. The Yeatman family went camping with another family who had a dog named Toasty. Toasty's famous trait – constantly humping people.

After a short pause, Ricky looked at Karen. "You are a wonderful, special, beautiful person," Ricky said gushing. Karen was the middle child with two older and two younger siblings. Everyone knew that she related with the "middle child syndrome." Knowing this, Bob made sure to let Karen know that he did not see her as just the middle child but a unique individual that he loved dearly.

"I'm seeing someone going south, the Carolina's or Florida. This is for work, but golfing as well. He is showing me a silver can, a Coors Light." Looking at Bobby, Ricky asked, "Do you ever go out on the golf course and have a beer and talk to your father while you are playing golf?"

"Yes," Bobby answered with a smile.

"When you go to Florida and you are out golfing, have a beer with your dad. (Bobby was leaving for Florida the following Tuesday.) Keep on talking to him, he hears you," Ricky said kindly. "He wishes he could still do that with you now," Ricky added. This brought fresh tears to Bobby's eyes. "But he's saying don't drink all the time," Ricky said in a warning manner. "Live every single minute of it. He wants you to be OK," Ricky said adamantly.

Turning towards Judy, Ricky said, "Your dad wants to sit you down. You are strong willed and you are not to be so hard on yourself and other people too. You have to have love, have love." Ricky said. "He wants you to talk to your brother more, the time will come up." Ricky said finishing that message. Judy did not show much emotion, congruent with her strong-willed personality, as her dad spoke to her through Ricky.

Your dad is saying, "He always felt like the center of attention with all of you. He is thanking all of you. Don't stop doing this with everybody and the kids here. This is the place to be." Ricky said.

"I see a bike ramp in the backyard, and a bike… doing tricks in the backyard." Ricky said looking at Bobby. "He's showing me this because you need validation that it is him," Ricky added. When Bobby was young, Bob had built him a bike ramp in their backyard.

"He knows you already believe," Ricky said looking at Debbie. "He's saying you tested his and your mom's nerves. He's acknowledging that you helped raise your sisters and brother." Ricky said matter-of-factly. Debbie smiled agreeing. She was the oldest so she always helped with the others. "You don't have to pay a penance anymore, you've learned quite well," Ricky said sincerely. Debbie knew what her dad was referring to and she cried as if he was saying it to her himself. At that moment she felt that her dad was there, talking to her lovingly and with a sincerity that she only felt with him. "He's saying only you could have pulled this off, Debbie. He is glad you all did this." Ricky said with a smile.

"I don't know what this is," Ricky said wrinkling his forehead. "I'm seeing Thomas the Train or Thomas the engine? The little engine that could," Ricky said finally feeling as though he got it. Collectively the family drew a breath in and for a moment you could have heard a pin drop. *The Little Engine That Could* was Bob's favorite story. They all remembered Bob telling them the classic line, "I think I can, I think I can." It was his biggest mantra to all of them on how to approach their lives. Most eyes in the room were moist remembering the times he had said this to them.

The more serious nature of Bob's messages came to an end, but he wasn't finished visiting. "I'm seeing rabbits and he's yelling about them. Two of you brought them in the house and they made a mess of the house," Ricky said smiling. Bob had helped build a bunny hutch in the backyard for his kids to have five rabbits. Judy and Bobby had brought two of them in the house and it had been a mess.

"Have any of your kids seen your dad since he passed?" Ricky asked. "Yes, our daughter Emma talks to him all the time," Denise said about her and Bobby's four-year-old-daughter.

"He's showing me pans that are hanging, frying pans, cast iron skillets in a place. I think it is the restaurant Cracker Barrel," Ricky said with a chuckle being fond of the restaurant himself. Cracker Barrel was the restaurant Bob and his family always ate at when they visited Judy in Virginia.

Ricky continued delivering messages. During this time, the scene in the family room was one of smiles and laughter with everyone finally relaxed and open. It was as if Bob and his family were all sitting around shooting the breeze. Bob had worked his magic again helping to turn a gathering into a party. He teased them, talked about times when they were growing up, and offered them more advice. Peacefulness had washed over everyone leaving them feeling as though they had been transported back to when Bob was still "alive."

For two hours, the Yeatman family was all together again. All of the sadness and grief had evaporated as quickly as a summer rain. The contentment was palpable.

When Ricky finished, he offered one last message privately. Asking Barb to step outside the room, he spoke with her in hushed tones for a few minutes. When they reemerged, Barb was visibly shaken as she sat back down. Concerned, her siblings asked, "Are you alright Barb?" *all right*

"Yeah, I'm alright, but he is the real thing. What he just told me, nobody knows."

"What is it?" they asked curiously.

"No, I'm not going to talk about it," Barb said still trying to regain her composure.

Ricky hung out for a long while afterwards. It was almost as if Bob didn't want it to end as much as his family. Each basked in the reunion, continuing the reminiscing for a long time afterward.

Although Bob Yeatman's family still misses his physical presence dearly, the reunion Ricky facilitated changed their lives. Even if just for two hours, they were able to gather with him once again and feel his contagious joyful nature. It was evident to everyone there that our spirits do live on carrying with them the love and joy experienced while living a life in a physical body. Bob Yeatman lives on in the hearts of all of those who love him.

Here is what Debbie has to say about her and her family's experience with Ricky:

"Although I've always had spiritual beliefs and thought that there was an afterlife, being that I am a nurse, I am the kind of person that likes to see "proof." This experience with Ricky gave me the evidence and "proof" I need to completely believe in the fact that our spirits live on. What an incredible reading it was! My father's personality and stories for each one of us were truly amazing! Ricky not only gave us stories, but gave each one of us insights for daily living from our dad. I felt Ricky truly left us as a friend and he will be receiving calls from us again."

Debbie Siple

Yeatman Family
Bottom left to right – Barbara, Debbie, Judy,
Karen, Baby Katie.
Middle Row left – Barb's husband Mike, Bobby
Jr., Bob Sr., Lucille.
Back Row left – Debbie's husband Michael,
Karen's husband Tim.

Robert "Bob" H. Yeatman

Q & A with Ricky

In this story, the family did not want to give you any "clues" to make sure you were giving them authentic information. During the reading you asked them to "work with you" to validate the information you were giving them. When people validate what you are saying, does it change the information you will get and give?

"No, it doesn't change the information I'm getting, it just takes a lot of energy to say things over and over again. If I was saying something for fifteen minutes that they didn't understand or get, I'm wasting their time."

So, if you are saying something and you are NOT getting validated (like in the beginning of this story) you just move on to the next thing. Could this possibly make you skip some information that could otherwise come through?

"I won't spend as much time on it, you know, I'll just move on to the next thing."

Is it more difficult for you to do a "group" or "gallery" reading than an "individual" reading?

"Sometimes a gallery reading seems easy and sometimes a one-on-one seems easy. I've had instances where I've sat down and felt like somebody took an AC plug and stuck it in my head and said, "Get Going!" I felt energized by it because whoever had passed had that type of personality. They didn't waste any time, they had a clear connection. There are times in a gallery read I get clearly, "Who had boom, and who had boom, and this is here." It really depends on my state of well-being, the mood I'm in, and how willing I am to receive. It isn't always in my best interest to do seven sessions in a row, and then the next morning do a gallery session. You know I need to sleep, eat, rest, and have fun like everybody else. I think sometimes people forget that."

During this gallery session, you would turn to each person and give them a message. Is it confusing when you get all of this information for different people?
   "No."

How do you know to go to that person? Are you pushed towards them? How do you know?
   "This particular family was very interesting. It was one of the few times where it came across like that. Like "You boom boom boom, you boom boom boom, and you," like this, Ricky said pointing."

How did you know it was for that person? Were you pushed to them?
   "Yes, I was pushed to point. I can't really explain it. It really is just what happened."

Do you feel your body move towards that person?
   "No, I don't want you to think something took control of me and said, "Move your feet this way."

I felt that the energy was directed at that person. Think about like this, if you are a mom and you have five kids, and you know that most likely the energy is little Joey. He is the one that broke that lamp. He's giving off some kind of energy. It wasn't like anyone in the gallery was giving off an energy; I felt something when I moved towards them. That's what it felt like."

What is it that you are "feeling" when you are being pulled towards that person?

"It is an awkward question to answer because most of the time I don't remember much afterwards. But I can tell you I remember being there and I was there for a while, a few hours. I do remember feeling that I needed to shut it down because I was exhausted. It was almost as if the father was giving his last words. This was his family so I felt like "And with you, make sure you brush your teeth, and with you make sure you walk the dog, and with you…." I felt that and it just comes out. There isn't a switch that comes on. It is kind of like….I don't know what it is like to tell you the truth. I didn't have a particular group of feelings. It isn't like my stomach swelled or my feet tingled. You know, when you are talking to someone and you are engaged in conversation with them and you want to be as articulate as you can and it is a good friend, conversation just keeps going and going. You get more and more into it. That's what it felt like. It felt like someone was talking and I was helping them have that conversation. I hope that answered your question."

Yes, thank you. When you were giving messages from Bob and then you expressed that other spirits were pushing through, like Barb's in-laws, how do you decipher who is coming through?

"I feel it. Look at it this way. Some people emote more on this planet like they give you parts of their personality. If it was a gay man he may be very flamboyant if that was him. You can feel a feminine energy. So usually, if those energies start to shift, I go wow this isn't the same person giving me the information anymore. It feels different. You know, if Uncle Bob was a rascally kind of guy and always joking around, but the person I've been communicating with is very stoic and very serious, it is different."

So you are pulled towards a person in the group and then you feel that it might be a parental figure like Barb?

"Sometimes I'll hear 'parent' or I'll hear 'dog.' It is almost as if you could keep your mind open and think of yourself as a receptacle. Your mind is a big open room and you've swept everything out then something appears in your mind. It is a dog. Then you get a feeling about the dog as you talk about it. The more I do this…. You could ask me two years from now; it could be different the way I get information. I have a dear friend from

Arizona, Holly Matthews, who does this work. When she does it, she gets more emoting, more feelings than facts. I've experienced that too. In other words, Uncle Frank might be so glad to see everyone and he is so excited to see everyone and he loves them so much! But you have to go wait a second, I have to get these people some facts, but he is just so excited to see him and he is all over the place. So I'll have to slow down a minute and go, 'well he is just an excitable guy.' Holly is the one who taught me to ask to switch frequencies or channels."

With switching "channels" do you mean "hearing" or "seeing" or how you get the information?
    "Think of them as frequencies like you can pick up CNN on channel 202 and pick up FOX on 404."

I don't understand. Do you mean switch channels to get different spirits?
    "To get different information."

Oh, you mean the same spirit is the whole radio but different channels are different information?
    "In other words, it might not be as clear on one station as it is on another."

Oh, OK. So you may be able to hear music on 98.2, but it is full of static. By rolling it down to 98.1 it is clear and you can hear it better.
    "Right, sorry to confuse you."

Now I get it. Ok, well next, when you say that spirits are pushing through, is that how it feels that they are vying to speak?

"Put it this way, think of a big barbeque. You've got all your relatives at the barbeque. There is Aunt Joan, and Aunt Missy, and Aunt Tolula, and then you've got your cousins Bob and Frank. They all have their own personalities and some are pushier than others. So let's say you are standing on the other side of the big picnic table and you said, "This tastes just like Grandma's chicken." And then someone yells from the other side, "That's not your grandmother's chicken! Your grandmother's chicken had ..." Then someone else puts their input in. Whoever has the loudest mouth wins."

That's how you decide who you are going to listen to, whoever is the loudest or strongest?

"Sometimes, it depends on the situation. If Grandmom was a very gentle and quiet woman, I have to struggle to pull that through. And if her sister is this larger presence and she keeps talking about the cat, and was much louder than Grandmom, and talking over her and Grandmom couldn't stand that. I'll have to ask them to stop so I can hear Grandmom. It is always dependent upon the individual spirits and their personalities."

15

A Few Final Questions

Q & A with Ricky

Throughout the book, you spoke frequently about a person's "belief system" being one of the major determining factors in what happens to them when they die. If someone doesn't have a specific "belief system" because they have not felt cohesiveness with a particular religion, or was even turned off by experiencing hypocrisy or judgment through religion, could you suggest a way to help them find or develop their own belief system?

"I don't know if I can tell them how to develop a belief system."

What tools could you use or steps to take if they want to build or strengthen a "belief system" and they don't have a specific religion or beliefs?

"Well, a belief system is not religion. So what I meant by that is whatever people believe about life and death. What *they* believe. If they believe that there is going to be someone waiting for them, then that is what will happen. That is a belief system, not a religious system."

Does that mean that you manifest what you believe will happen?

"Right. If you believe that you are dead and there is nothing but darkness, you may be walking around in the dark until hopefully a relative or someone who knows you grabs you and says, 'Over here.' You know whether it is the sun that someone is connected to, whether it is the light, whether it is Catholicism, its spiritual – the movement of the spirit, whatever you believe about spirit. For some people the difference between religion and spirituality is that 'religion was made for people who were afraid of going to hell, spirituality is for people who have already been there.'"

Did you make that statement up?

"No, I overheard it somewhere."

If you don't need to have a religious affiliation to have a "belief system" then can it just come from a place of love or caring with a person, animal, or even nature as long as you feel love?

"Love is the magnet. Love is the magnet that attracts us. And for those who don't feel love very much in their lives, somewhere along the line they had something. It might have been their pet. It could be a cowboy that lived by himself out in the desert and his horse meant everything to him. Something that is connected with love and caring will be what helps carry you over."

It seems then that the desert and his horse could be the cowboy's eternity?

"That's not what I meant. I'll use another example to clarify what I meant. Let's say that Jack Smith from 1872 was an orphan, lived on his own, and didn't have much around him and then he died. But that horse that he had always stuck by him. If he had sugar in his pocket, he would give it to his horse before he would put it in his own coffee. He loved that horse and that horse was kind to him. Most likely he'll see a picture of that horse that'll bring him to the light."

Do you personally think that religious affiliations are beneficial for people, their belief systems, and their efforts to be more loving, caring, and giving? If so, Why?

"Yes, absolutely. I think anything that brings people together for worship is wonderful. If it brings forth prayer it is truly great because prayer is a wonderful thing. Religions all seem to have very similar doctrines: treat others as you would like to be treated, forgive, all of those things are wonderful. I think that we are all ok with that."

If someone asked you for help in preparing to make a smooth transition to the after-life, what advice would you give them?

"Pack lightly. One bag or you'll get charges and stuff. (Chuckle) What I would say is that I wish in western culture we did more to prepare for death."

Yes, you said that previously, so what advice would you give people to help others prepare as well as themselves?

"In helping others, talk to people. If you are with Grandpa and he's dying, assure him that Grandma will be there. Let them know not to fear, that it is just a transition. Look for light. Look for love. Feel the love."

From what you said, I've surmised that there is not a huge difference from being 'alive' in a physical body and not, except for the physical aspect experienced through the human body. Would it be correct to say that we as humans over emphasize physical experience and death, therefore losing the connection to our never ending or eternal spiritual nature?

"What?" (Laughter by all)

Do you think that because we put such an emphasis on the physical aspect of us more so than the spiritual that may be the reason many of us have felt so crushed by a loved ones "death"?

"I would say there are some societies that are better suited for death. If you love someone and you are used to touching them, but you can't touch them or hug them anymore, it is absolutely natural to feel grief and to grieve. You move through that.

It is very difficult to say, 'Hey, don't worry about it, you'll see them soon.'"

I understand that, but isn't the key realizing that someone you loved and lost, isn't really lost? They aren't gone forever; there is still a connection with them. They are probably right there at moments when they are needed.

"It's good to know we still have that connection, but we are human too. Look, if your best friend who you love and has been by your side forever decided to pack and go to a remote village in Uruguay for fifteen years and once in a while you get a little message, you're still going to miss them. But it is ok, because you know that in fifteen years they will be flying back to Cleveland or wherever you are. I'm saying that I think missing people is absolutely normal, and I think sometimes we try to avoid it. You know, missing them starts the connection. If you didn't miss anybody, you wouldn't notice they weren't there. It would be no big deal."

I know, but I think my main goal was to speak to people who are in excruciating pain and unable to move on with their life after the loss of a loved on. I hope that they could find something in this book that would click with them so they will be able to have less pain.

"I think that, honestly, all the questions you ask I'm going to answer with the letter 'Q.' (Smile and pause) If you believe strongly enough and I don't mean "I BELIEVE" gritting your teeth, but more like they're ok. Radiate love and you'll get the love back. That's the best form of communication I've ever felt -- that if you radiate love you will get it back."

Whatever you give you'll get back.

"Right. Sometimes they'll do it through songs; sometimes they'll do it through a TV show. For whatever reason, that really weird song that you very rarely ever hear on the radio, and you are in your car and you are having a sad day, and you hear that Pina colada song, and you turn it up real loud because nobody is in the car with you, but it is your favorite person's song. Sing along, they'll be singing with you."

This is my very last question. What final words would you say to those reading this who may be looking for peace from the loss of a loved one, trying to come to terms with their own immortality, or just trying to better understand the big picture?

"Q. That's my final answer, Q. You've already asked all those questions. So my answer is Q."

Thank you. I really appreciate all of your time and insight. All laced with your wonderful sense of humor and a heart of gold. Thank you Ricky Wood.

As I was finishing this book – I was reading *The Power of Now* by Eckhart Tolle. This one sentence from this must read seemed to sum it up for me – pg. 197 –

> *"Nothing that was ever real died, only names, forms, and illusions."*

Ricky Wood's office locations --
PA Address
1055 Westlakes Drive Suite 300
Berwyn, PA 19312

AZ Address
60 East Rio Salado Parkway Suite 900
Tempe, AZ 85281

Phone - 484-459-5489
Email- bchboy@rickywood.net
Visit his website at www.RickyWood.net.

Breinigsville, PA USA
04 December 2009
228628BV00003B/8/P